real food real kitchens
NEW YORK
COOKBOOK

real food real kitchens
NEW YORK
COOKBOOK
CRAIG CHAPMAN

FRONT TABLE BOOKS | AN IMPRINT OF CEDAR FORT, INC. | SPRINGVILLE, UTAH

© 2015 Craig Chapman
Photography by Jammi York, except where credited otherwise
Real Food Real Kitchens Executive Producer Jonah McMichael
Recipe Development and Testing Davon Hines
All rights reserved.

ISBN 13: 978-1-4621-1724-6

Published by Front Table Books, an imprint of Cedar Fort, Inc.
2373 W. 700 S., Springville, UT 84663
Distributed by Cedar Fort, Inc., www.cedarfort.com

LIBRARY OF CONGRESS CATALOGING-IN-PUBLICATION DATA

Chapman, Craig, 1974-
  Real food, real kitchens : New York cookbook / Craig Chapman.
    pages cm
  ISBN 978-1-4621-1724-6 (layflat binding : alk. paper)
  1. International cooking. 2. Cooking--New York (State)--New York. 3.
Cooks--New York (State)--New York. I. Title.
  TX725.A1C5235 2015
  641.59747--dc23
                              2015019333

Cover and page design by M. Shaun McMurdie
Cover design © 2015 by Lyle Mortimer
Edited by Melissa J. Caldwell

Printed in China

10 9 8 7 6 5 4 3 2 1

Printed on acid-free paper

Dedicated to my mother and father,
Bernice and Phil Chapman

I LOVE YOU!

CONTENTS

FOREWORDS

REAL FOOD REAL KITCHENS: NEW YORK

Regina A. Bernard-Carreño, PhD

When Craig introduced me to his digital work (*Real Food Real Kitchens*: the show) and then his current cookbook project, I think I breathed an immediate and audible sigh of relief. *Here it is,* I thought, *a book about family that I can actually imagine and envision; with food that I can recognize!* So much of the popular and in-circulation within the intellectual genre around food seems foreign to me, and probably to many other people. I'm even more skeptical and disheartened when said materials are about New York City. While reading or watching it, I am, of course, intrigued, but I don't feel at home.

From our first exchange of chatter through email, I knew I would be more than excited to participate in his project, and I am so honored that he asked me to write for it too. Reading through his book, and engaging him in conversation about "family, food, culture, and history" as he outlines it, finally felt like I was placing my hardcore and overly passionate attempts at preserving authenticity in good hands. Craig has been able to capture personal memories, life stories, and narratives of lived experiences that are so important to the history of my beloved city, New York.

As I moved from one family to the next in the *Real Food Real Kitchens* cookbook, I became more and more attached to their stories, because many of them had elements of familiarity. Growing up as the only American-born child in a biracial Guyanese family with no other Guyanese contact outside of our family, my mother's delicacies and carefully crafted handiwork in the kitchen felt like our entire family's secret. In many of the essays, Craig draws out beautiful stories, secrets, and memories told by the very people it should be told by. There are such endless social dynamics, struggles, and upkeep endured by families all over just to get through the day, that it was heartwarming to read that so many of them still join together and eat at the "family table." When meals are presented at that "family table," there are no surprises, no worry, or hesitation about what's about to hit your plate. Your curiosity only wonders whether it will taste as good as "the last time mom made it," and it usually does. The comfort of many of the dishes presented in the *Real Food Real Kitchens* cookbook almost jumped off the table they were served on, and right out of the book.

I flipped through the *Real Food Real Kitchens* cookbook and began seeing how many dishes I could identify just by their pictures alone. Quizzing myself at every turn, I wondered if that picture was Sancocho or what kind of curry powder was used for the Chicken Curry. The dishes I didn't recognize, I wanted to try, and as I always do, I started to fantasize about the dish's cultural history. The meals I positively guessed right on the first try, I read those stories even closer, sometimes more than once. I wanted to know how that dish played a role in their family's version of togetherness. The book introduced me to people I had never met, yet they were so familiar. Growing up in Hells Kitchen, NYC, and reflecting on that time while I read through the narratives and recipes in the *Real Food Real Kitchens* cookbook made me realize again that many of us linguistically, culturally, racially, and perhaps even socioeconomically here in New York City, are separated by just a few dining tables. Despite our vast differences, however, we all still eat. Someone is making that food, and it has a history and a narrative.

Especially warm did it make me feel to read all the Caribbean/West Indian narratives in this book. Craig's construction and research for the book didn't funnel or pigeon-hole people into the places where they necessarily live now or what he needed them to be. He allowed families to reflect on where they originally came from before coming to New York. A great example is in the "Queens" section, and the story of Ethel. Although she lives in Queens now, he understood that her food narrative after leaving Guyana, really firmly began in Manhattan, circa 1960s. He wanted to hear that story and the stories prior to that point of immigration which led her now to reflecting in this way, and from this place. The questions asked of her stirred memories of being in two places and generated whispers among her three children about their own memories, ones that were safely compartmentalized somewhere other than here. There's no more focus on authenticity than letting a story be told naturally without makeup for scripted purposes.

Craig shows a real and sincere commitment to storytelling, and I am so glad he put this book together. I hope that many will find comfort and joy in the pages ahead, just as I have.

Marie A. Bragg, PhD

Craig Chapman's *Real Food Real Kitchens* documentary series introduces a new dynamic to modern-day cooking shows. Rather than solely focusing on showing viewers how to make a few different components to a meal, Chapman uses food as an avenue to share cultures and identities and to emphasize the importance of tradition and family to bring people around the dinner table. His new cookbook, bearing the same name, takes on a similar approach and empowers readers with the tools to try out new recipes from families around the five boroughs of New York City. Readers and viewers alike are introduced to traditional and non-traditional chefs who enjoy cooking meals passed down to them from family members. They also share stories, often about how they became interested in cooking, while giving some history about the recipes of the foods they are sharing. Some come from families of a long line of chefs, while others are simply mothers who prefer to use cooking as an escape from a hectic day. Additionally, readers are invited into the homes and kitchens of New Yorkers. There is something truly unique about the way *Real Food Real Kitchens* goes inside the homes of everyday people to hear their story in a setting familiar to

them, inviting readers and viewers to be part of a meal that is more often than not of longtime tradition.

One aspect of the cookbook that I personally enjoy involves the families who use cooking as a means of bonding with both friends and family. Today, it is quite common for people to skip cooking and jump straight to the eating—often through pre-prepared meals or dining outside of the home. This cookbook, like the TV show, demonstrates how people are returning to their roots through this increasingly common trend to cook cherished, traditional meals to enjoy with others. Some families even share stories on how they venture to the market or supermarket to purchase fresh produce and meats that typically enhance the taste of the food.

I am a professor at the NYU School of Medicine, and my research focuses on how the processed food industry has contributed to obesity by driving families away from traditional home cooking and pushing them toward consumption of cheap, highly processed foods that are high in sugar, salt, and fat. It is alarming how quickly and easily those foods contribute to weight gain, diabetes, and high blood pressure. So, as an avid researcher in the realm of food choice and dietary decisions, I commonly encounter instances where people are surprised by how much cheaper their meals are when they are home cooked. By shopping for fresh meats and produce, consumers have more control over what they eat, not to mention getting more bang for their buck in eliminating labor costs and long food shipping miles that contribute to damaging the environment. Indeed, cooking at home is a win for our bodies, a win for our relationships with others, and a win for the environment. Craig Chapman's cookbook brings those realities to life.

Home-cooked meals are not only cheaper but are also healthier in the physical and emotional sense. My training as a clinical psychologist has convinced me of the importance spending time with friends, family, and even neighbors has on health. Eating, in the traditional aspect, has always been an activity shared in a group or in pairs. Now, more than ever, people are seen eating alone or snacking, often consuming unhealthy foods at a fast pace. This is in part due to conflicting, hectic schedules preventing people the opportunity to sit down and eat together. However, as seen in *Real Food Real Kitchens*, cooking can be used as a tool to bring family and friends together around a table like the good ol'

days. Much of the currently available research and "quick studies" seen on news outlets demonstrate that cooking a meal consisting of fresh produce and meat can be done more quickly (and more cost effectively) than getting drive-thru at your nearest fast food restaurant. Cooking requires knowledge of what exactly goes in a meal, which requires preparation, including the amount of time it's going to take and the necessary ingredients. Although this may seem like a lot, it is fairly simple and almost always informs families of the nutrients they are consuming—something that does not always come so easily when eating processed or premade foods. The accounts in *Real Food Real Kitchens* exemplify how simple cooking at home can be and how enjoyable it is for families to share some of their traditions, or the traditions of others, through food.

When I think about events or occasions when my family comes together, food is at the center of everything. I come from a rather large family where our Trinidadian history is very important and passed down from generation to generation. Like many of those featured in the cookbook, I learned to cook from my parents and grandparents, who learned from their parents and grandparents. Our family loves the traditional foods of our culture, and we look forward to eating them at family gatherings. In the *Real Food Real Kitchens* cookbook, many individuals developed the same passion for cooking that their family members before them did. Some even see the same passion and willingness to learn in their children, who also enjoy cooking traditional and nontraditional meals for their family. Food is central to the family. It's what has always brought the family together and an aspect of life that will continue to bring the family together. As one cook from the show put it, food keeps the family and the memories alive—an important concept for many of the cookbook's featured New Yorkers.

With obesity and other chronic diseases plaguing the world, a cookbook of this nature is an important if not critical step toward making Americans healthy again. Many in the public health sector blame this worldwide obesity epidemic on the types of foods that have become most common in the last few decades: fast food, processed foods, sugar-sweetened beverages, and sugary snacks. As a society, we have become more reliant on foods low in nutrition because they are more easily and readily available compared to the healthy, nutritious foods that take more time to prepare. As Michael Pollan says, "Eat food. Not too much. Mostly plants." This simplistic recipe to healthy, nutritious eating begins with people getting back into their own kitchens and cooking meals from scratch. Whether you're looking to read great stories about modern-day families living in the New York City area or find delicious recipes to make at your next family dinner, you've come to the right place. The *Real Food Real Kitchens* cookbook is for bookworms, foodies, and chefs alike.

INTRODUCTION

REAL FOOD REAL KITCHENS: NEW YORK

Craig Chapman

Real Food Real Kitchens prides itself on four words: family, food, culture, and history. These four words sum up what *Real Food Real Kitchens* is all about. The idea is to tell the story of a dish and the family and culture that bring it to life. Early on I decided to start the description of the brand with the word *family* instead of *food* for a reason. The word *family* is intended to be all-inclusive, not defined in the traditional sense of the word. After all, everyone finds family in a different place and in different ways. I like to define *family* as those around a person that make him or her feel at home, loved, relaxed, and at peace. It could be mom and dad and children and grandmas and grandpas and brothers and sisters. But sometimes family is found elsewhere—a newlywed couple, two best friends living on their own for the first time, a group of college students living away from home. You can find family in your neighbors, your pets, or even within your community. No matter what conglomerate you call "family," the next thing that brings us all together as one family is food, and food is the exciting part of *Real Food Real Kitchens*.

Food is the soul of all living things. It's the one thing we must all have; it's the one thing we all have in common—we must eat. Sitting down to eat with one another is the time when we can set aside the stresses of the day, the conflicts, the disagreements, and really share an indescribable moment. Put some good food on the table, and for a moment all the problems of the world have been solved. Cooking and sharing food with one another is the purest expression of love. Within the pages of this book, you will find that one commonality among all of the at-home chefs and "families" featured on each page. Not only are they sharing their memories connected to food and certain dishes, but they also are sharing a recipe that has filled them with love, one that they use to show love to their families in return. What an amazing thing to share with all of us— such an intimate moment, such a personal part of life, shared selflessly with us, complete strangers to the guests in this book.

Culture and history almost go hand in hand. As the world continues to change and we get increasingly busier, as has happened for past generations, preserving these recipes—pieces of our culture and history—is becoming more vital. I've heard the same phrase so many times since starting *Real Food Real Kitchens*: "My family member passed away without ever writing that recipe down on paper. It was always locked away in his or her mind, and the thing I miss the most about him or her which makes me the most sad is that I will never taste that dish quite the same ever again. That love is lost forever." So I made it my mission to create *Real Food Real Kitchens* as a way for us to all contribute and preserve these cultural family recipes for generations to come, long after we are gone. There has not been one guest on the *Real Food Real Kitchens* TV show, in the magazine, or in this book that hasn't welled up with tears while telling their food and family stories. So having this space to document these stories is important to us, us as *Real Food Real Kitchens* and all of us as individuals.

Tracking the history of these dishes is the final fascinating piece to *Real Food Real Kitchens*. It's amazing to see that no matter how far we are apart geographically that we all have some similarities in our food. Sure we have different spices and different ingredients, but we all have some sort of stew, bread, or sauce that we all make. The history of these dishes, while only touched on in

this book, is another fascinating aspect of *Real Food Real Kitchens* that should be explored on its own.

I chose New York City as the focus of the first *Real Food Real Kitchens* book for obvious reasons. It's the greatest city on earth! While I am not a native, I have spent the past twenty years calling it home and exploring as much of it as I can. What I love most are the people and how many different stories there are just waiting to be told inside the walls of each building, the walls that its inhabitants call home and the walls and stories that make up this vast metropolis. Native New Yorkers have great stories of arriving in this country through New York Harbor and have generations of family living within the neighborhoods and blocks that make up each borough. You will find many of these generational stories within these pages. New York is also where people come to make dreams come true so you will find people from all over the world that moved to New York to follow their dreams. They have brought with them some incredible recipes and have created homes in the many different neighborhoods in the city. They have met new friends and created families in the welcoming city of New York, a city where there is a place for everyone. I was one of these souls, and I smile while writing this because of the memories, both good and bad, that I have made in

New York. Almost all of these memories include food—some with familiar flavors, but most with unfamiliar flavors I am always excited to try.

While this book only tells just a few of the thousands of stories within New York, my hope is it becomes a starting point for many more installations of this cookbook series to come. I hope this book gets us all around the table at home with our loved ones we call family and friends. Thank you for sharing.

BROOKLYN | NEW YORK

Brooklyn is currently at its height on the foodie forefront. Everyone looks to Brooklyn for "what's next" in food. What Brooklynites get that others don't is the "what's next" in Brooklyn has turned into "what was" in Brooklyn back when it had gardens, food purveyors, and locally sourced ingredients. Brooklynites are getting back to the basics of simply good food. What better way to do this than to look within to find out what makes up the fabric of Brooklyn—the flavors and people that were and are Brooklyn. Pockets of comfort and home lie around every corner in this borough, and behind every dimly lit window is a story of family, food, culture, and history from decades past to current day. Brooklyn's flavors reflect the diversity of its people, who offer an endless exploration of tastes from all over the world.

NEW
YORK

ADA CORCINO

BUSHWICK / EAST WILLIAMSBURG, BROOKLYN

{ *Dominican* }

Ada's recipe and story are a great example what *Real Food Real Kitchens* is all about: family, food, culture, and history. She moved to Brooklyn in the 1980s but actually grew up in the Dominican Republic. "We are from the Dominican Republic. I grew up in a small community there called Batey Libertad where most of my family members stayed. I then moved to a town called Esperanza minutes away." She learned to cook very early in life from her mother. "I started cooking when I was seven in order to help my mom who would cook food to sell to workers nearby. I never read a recipe, and I am able to put dishes together that taste great by just eyeballing it because that's how my mom taught me." She continues to reflect on some of her first memories of cooking with her mother. "My favorite memory was when I caught my first fish. There was a big river behind my house, and back when I was growing up it had a lot of fish so I would go back there to try to catch some. One day I finally caught some with my hands and then cooked them with my mom."

Ada decided to share a Dominican Sancocho, which is like a stew or soup with different root vegetables and meats that she grew up on. "My mom taught me how to cook it when I was younger." There are many variations of the dish, which first originated in Cuba. Sancocho is a popular dish not only because it is delicious, but also because it's inexpensive and easy to make. "My family is so big that we had to find a way to feed everyone on a budget. Sancocho is a dish that does just that. Living in a country where most people grow their own food, we had to use what we had. It is very filling and also tastes good. It was also a big part of our celebration days. We would have a huge pot on a wood fire and everyone would take turns stirring or making sure it didn't burn."

Sancocho, for Ada today, is a great representation of the multicultural neighborhood of Bushwick/ East Williamsburg, Brooklyn, where she lives. To her, making Sancocho is "like a bonding experience because there's so many ingredients. We all have to help out to make it. My neighborhood is very diverse. In my building, there are a lot of Spanish people from all over. Once you step outside, it's another story. With the gentrification process, you see a lot of Americans, which is something you didn't see when I arrived here back in the '80s. They are also called hipsters and have changed the dynamic of the area with a lot of pop up shops, art shows, and restaurants that I never imagined seeing. Just a block away, you find Knickerbocker Avenue where you find people from Mexico, DR, and Puerto Rico. On the warmer days you can find food carts in the streets with the smell of kebabs and empanadas as well as shaved ice carts." Sounds like a beautiful mixture of old and new cultures, traditions, and food . . . like a bubbling pot of Sancocho on Ada's stovetop. Delicious!

(l to r) Martha Palacios, Ada Corcino, Dawin Polanco, Maria Corcino, Frances Duran, Wilber Polanco, Justina Cruz-Corsino

Dominican Sancocho

Serves 9 to 13 people

"Here is the recipe: Authentic Dominican Sancocho. Why authentic? Because it comes from the country where we used all the natural ingredients, which are healthy and tasty. You can also alternate the meat that you want to put in it." — Ada

2 lbs. of beef shank with bones

1 whole chicken

1 tsp. oregano, divided

Salt to taste

1½ tsp. black pepper, split

6 garlic cloves, chopped and divided

1 sour orange or lemon

1 onion, sliced

1 green pepper, sliced

13½ cups water, divided

½ tsp. thyme

2 lbs. pork, optional

1 stem celery

3 green plantains

1 lb. yellow yautia

1 lb. white yautia

1 lb. cassava (yucca)

1 lb. yams

1½ lbs. Caribbean pumpkin (you can use buttercup or butternut squash as a substitute)

3 tsp. chopped cilantro

On the side: 2 lbs. white rice and 2 avocados

DIRECTIONS

1. Season the beef and chicken with oregano, salt, pepper, garlic, and sour orange or lemon. Let marinate 15–20 minutes.

2. Brown and cook the beef and chicken for 30 minutes separately. Then add to a large pot.

3. Sauté onion, garlic, and peppers in a pan for about 2 minutes. Add 1½ cups water and boil, stirring and scraping up brown bits for about 1 minute.

4. Transfer vegetable mixture to pot. Add thyme, 2 teaspoons salt, ½ teaspoon pepper, and remaining 12 cups water to pot, and let it boil for about 1½ hours.

5. Peel all the vegetables and cut them into 1¼-inch pieces.

6. Take out the seeds from the pumpkin. It is okay if the pumpkin gets very soft—it will add more flavor and color to the Sancocho.

7. Add all the vegetables to the pot and boil for about 30 minutes more or until vegetables are soft, stir occasionally. Add cilantro while water is boiling.

8. Water should thicken and become soupy. If needed, you can add more water.

9. Serve with rice and avocados. Enjoy!

MARIE BRAGG

WILLIAMSBURG, BROOKLYN

{ *Trinidadian* }

Williamsburg, Brooklyn—perhaps the hippest most hipster neighborhood in the United States. Gentrified decades ago, Williamsburg is the epicenter of hipster-dom, the forefront of everything "cool": music, art, fashion, and, yes, food.

Marie lives in South Williamsburg and loves all of these characteristics the neighborhood has to offer and more. "Williamsburg has a lot of young people who blend together to look like young, hip families composed of people from all over the globe. I love the diversity of restaurants, local coffee shops, and the combination of residents who are either sporting lots of tattoos and piercings or pushing their kids around in strollers (often it's both tattoos and strollers) or just hanging out in the park playing frisbee or bocce ball or some random game that was clearly just made up that day. Food ranges from the most amazing barbecue at Fette Sau or some southern comfort food, like corn bread and deviled eggs at Extra Fancy, to health-conscious pressed juices and locally sourced dishes inspired by produce from local farmers markets. On the weekends, Smorgasburg draws enormous crowds to its market, which specializes in vendors who make handcrafted jewelry and home goods along with really creative food vendors that sell everything from hot dogs with crushed potato chips on top to hibiscus-flavored donuts."

Coming to the home of Marie and her fiancé, Tom, you quickly learn there's a wealth of cultural and social influence at the heart of their lives. "We live in South Williamsburg, Brooklyn, but our family is originally from Trinidad. My sister Alexandra and I grew up in Florida, and we both moved to New York within the past couple of years to work at NYU in the area of public health. I'm a professor at NYU School of Medicine, and she's a lab coordinator for HealthRight International,

which focuses on helping marginalized communities (e.g. survivors of abuse and single mothers) get better access to healthcare and other services. My fiancé, Tom, grew up on Long Island and works as a middle school math teacher in the NYC public school system."

The one thing Marie hasn't lost to the modern, hipster world of Williamsburg is her cultural connection to food, especially when her sister is around. "Tonight we made traditional Trinidadian food prepared the way our great-grandmother, grandmother, and mother taught us to make it. The appetizer is oxtail soup with peas and potatoes; the main dish is salt fish and bake. The salt fish is salted cod, tomatoes, onions, and garlic with olive oil and salt and pepper, and the bake is fried dough that can be prepared plain or with meat or cheese inside. We also made coo-coo, which is a side dish like a casserole that's made with cornmeal and okra and coconut milk. Every Sunday growing up, our whole family would get together to make dishes like these. It's funny because even though all the women in my family used the same ingredients, you could pick out who made what each week because there were slight variations in sweetness or spiciness."

These traditional dishes are ones that draw up fragrant memories for Marie. "These weekend meals with my family were always my favorite. Looking at my sisters and mother through sleepy eyes, I would drink in the familiar Sunday morning scene. I wondered if the steel band music my mother played on the stereo was meant to be a friendly alarm clock or cruel joke. Either way, the clanging beat set a festive mood. My sisters and I ate salt fish and bake while my mother danced and sang as she cooked. The fried bake was a sort of fluffy, sweet dough, and taking a bite of a big piece always warmed me to my bones. Extended family members trickled in to help prepare lunch." These experiences influenced Marie for a lifetime and instilled in her a sense of pride and a wealth of knowledge about her Trinidadian heritage through food.

Like most families in Brooklyn, Marie's family immigrated to the United States for more opportunities in education and employment. "Our family left Trinidad in the 1980s or so to come to Florida. My siblings and I were born in Florida, but we grew up hearing stories about how challenging life could be in a developing country and how hard our family worked to be able to provide for us." She reinforces her connection to her past through food by saying, "These meals are our connection to that past and a real reminder of the importance of staying connected to that culture."

Aside from being an enormous part of her cultural background, food is also a large part of Marie's professional life as a professor at NYU School of Medicine. "My research focuses on food policy and obesity. Unfortunately, highly processed and packaged foods are replacing locally sourced, fresh ingredients, and major multinational food and beverage corporations promote products that are really unhealthy and hold little to no nutritional value. I would love if our research helped inspire people to move away from highly processed foods to finding more balance and creating time to cook in the kitchen with friends. It would help solve a lot of our problems with obesity, diabetes, and maltreatment of animals."

As Marie enjoys a night of food with family and close friends (one of her favorite things to do), she shares the importance of preserving and sharing these traditional recipes with them and the readers of this book: "My siblings and I are the first generation born in the United States. We run the risk of losing connection with where we came from and the values that helped our parents and grandparents get here. I remember my mom telling me stories about what it was like to be hungry, and I mean actually hungry, when she was a kid in Trinidad. She worked hard to make sure that I always had access to healthy foods. Years from now when my mom, aunts, uncles, and grandmother are gone, cooking their recipes will be the closest I can get to their warm embrace." A sentiment almost every human being on earth can relate to.

TOP (l to r) Marie Bragg, Arne Bostrom, Jen Goodman, Dustin Duncan, Alex Bragg, Tom Minnigan

Oxtail Soup

2 (16-oz.) packages fatty oxtail

1 (6-oz.) package Manischewitz soup mix

½ tsp. baking soda

1 large onion sliced

1 large tomato sliced

1 clove of garlic smashed

5 small red potatoes, cut into small cubes

3 large carrots, cut into chunks

2 ripe plantains, cut into chunks

1 Tbsp. salt

½ cup ketchup

3 beef or chicken bullion cubes

Pepper or hot sauce

DIRECTIONS

1. Simmer oxtail, soup mix, and baking soda in 7 cups of water for approximately two hours.

2. When the meat begins to come off the bone, add red potatoes and simmer for 30 more minutes until potatoes are soft.

3. Add carrots and remaining ingredients and simmer for another 10–20 minutes or until carrots are soft.

4. Add a dash of pepper or hot sauce to taste.

Salt Fish

1 lb. salt fish (normally comes in a box)

3 large tomatoes, diced

1 large onion, diced

1 clove garlic, diced

½ cup olive oil

pepper or hot sauce (optional)

DIRECTIONS

1. Cover fish in water and bring to a boil.

2. Remove from heat and pour fish into a colander. Strain and then rinse fish gently in cool water.

3. Let the fish completely cool and then shred by hand into bite-sized pieces.

4. Mix the fish with the rest of the ingredients in a large bowl by hand.

5. Add pepper or hot sauce to taste.

Bake

1 tsp. sugar

1 cup warm water, split in half

2 (.25-oz.) packages yeast

6 cups unsifted unbleached flour

½ stick butter

½ tsp. baking powder

DIRECTIONS

1. In a small bowl, add sugar to ½ cup warm water and then add yeast. Let this sit in warm area until yeast activates.

2. Meanwhile, mix flour, butter, and baking soda until butter is thoroughly mixed.

3. Add yeast to flour mix.

4. Slowly add extra warm water to flour until dough is slightly sticky (it might be more or less than ½ cup).

5. Mix by hand into ball. (Leave lumps in! Do not overknead.) When mixed well, cover with kitchen towel and place in warm area until dough rises.

6. Once dough has risen, knead again until smooth.

7. Break off small quarter-sized pieces and use a rolling pin to flatten them out.

8. Fry flattened pieces in hot peanut oil, flipping when bubbles rise on dough, about 10–15 seconds per side.

9. Place cooked pieces on a paper towel to cool before serving.

CooCoo

3 cups water

1 (16-oz.) package frozen or fresh okra

1 (13.5-oz.) can coconut milk

2 cups yellow cornmeal

2 sticks butter

1 (16-oz.) package of bacon, cut up and fried

DIRECTIONS

1. Bring water to a boil.

2. Add okra and cook until tender.

3. Add coconut milk.

4. Slowly add cornmeal. Stir using a whisk.

5. Add butter ½ stick at a time.

6. Add bacon.

7. Reduce heat to simmer and continue stirring using a whisk to avoid lumps.

8. Cook for approximately 4 minutes after bacon is added. Mixture should be thick (almost like thick mashed potatoes) but appear moist. Cooking too long will dry out the mixture.

JULIAN JOHN VASQUEZ

CARROLL GARDENS, BROOKLYN

{ *Italian* }

Julian loves to cook! Like many Italian children, Julian found home in the kitchen next to his mother and grandmother learning the ropes. "I learned how to cook most dishes by watching and asking questions. But when I really wanted to know how to make a dish, the answer was always a phone call away. Favorites like spaghetti, garlic and oil, pan-fried chicken cutlets, oven roasted chicken with potatoes, oregano and lemon, Sunday sauce, Grandma Josephine's pan pizza, and Mama Kay's Sicilian salad . . . I can go on and on and on. My roots of what I love to eat and cook come from my grandmothers like all good Italian boys! But I've also worked and still work in the food business, so I was able to find a more concrete foundation to food and cooking and the ability to learn more about dishes from all parts of Italy. Italian is my favorite to cook and eat. I love the simplicity, but what is most important to how I cook is finding the best ingredients to express the purity of flavors."

Today as a grown man with his own family, Julian has brought those traditional, homemade Italian dishes in to his own home in Carroll Gardens, Brooklyn. He attributes his amazing cooking skills to his great-grandparents, who first came to New York from Italy. "My family and I currently live in Carroll Gardens. My parents both grew up in Bushwick, Brooklyn, and I was born and raised predominantly in Queens. We lived in Ozone Park and Woodhaven, with a stint in Long Island. My grandparents are also from Brooklyn . . . it was my great-grandparents who came from across the ocean. My mother's side is from Sicily, Italy, and my dad's side is from Campania, Italy, and Castilla, Spain."

Carroll Gardens, Brooklyn, is traditionally an Italian-American neighborhood for generations. Julian finds it easy to call this neighborhood home. "This is a perfect marriage for a neighborhood. Carroll Gardens still has a good bunch of American Italians here. You still hear the language spoken by the older generation all the time. There's also lots of Italian specialty stores, bakeries, butchers, and cheese and wine shops. You can always smell fresh bread and cookies baking at all hours. There's even a coffee shop that's been around for about one hundred years, and they roast in house. Love the smell of coffee! Everyone is friendly in the neighborhood, especially the old-school families, but of course it takes some time for them to warm up to you. The advantage I have with how I establish my relationships with all the Italians in the hood is my roots, being a New Yorker and coming from an Italian background. It's also a good thing I speak the their language—food! The neighborhood is changing, though, with an influx of French and, of course, random Americans. So, slowly that is shaping what Carroll Gardens will become. I love this neighborhood because it feels like the ones I grew up in Queens, particularly Ozone Park."

Out of the hundreds of classic Italian dishes he's learned to cook over the years, Julian picked just one to share with us, and for good reason. "Today I made a dish called 'Italian Wedding Soup,' also known as escarole and meatball soup. It's a classic Italian dish that is more associated with American Italians nowadays. The dish actually has nothing to do with weddings but more with the marriage of flavors. This is a dish that my grandmother, Mama Kay, made traditionally on Christmas Day and Easter Sunday. I made it for my kids once, and it is now a staple in our house. We eat it more than two times a year! I think every time I make it, it's a holiday in our house."

Julian's fondest memories of childhood all revolve around his extended family gathering to eat, memories he hopes to pass on to his own children one day. "[I remember most] my family getting together for the holidays and on Sundays. Lots of cousins, aunts, uncles of many generations. We would see each other every Sunday at my grandmother Mama Kay's house (my mom's mom). We would eat right at 2:00 p.m. until it was time to go! We would be there so long we could take naps! The apartment was so small, but somehow there would be a minimum of twenty-five people at the house breaking bread."

Preserving family dishes is a long-term instillation that Julian has slowly started to introduce to his own children. "I try to get my kids interested in cooking, but I don't force it. They enjoy getting their hands dirty when I make bread, pizza, or fresh pasta. Soon they will be rolling out the meatballs. But they always seem to want to help when it comes to baking cookies or anything sweet. They can't wait to lick the batter out of the bowl. Preserving family dishes is so important, more for the tradition that

they have. We might not get together anymore like we used to every Sunday when I was kid, but I hope my children will make this soup on Christmas and Easter. I hope they continue to make and eat seafood (the feast of the seven fishes) on Christmas Eve, and have lentils and sausage on New Year's Eve. I look forward to seeing my children grow up and having them over with their friends and their families every Sunday. I want them to know what that feels like. People need to be reminded how special it is to enjoy the company of your family not just on special occasions. There is no better way to make memories than breaking bread and sipping wine with the ones you love!"

At the end of the day, even with his vast knowledge of Italian food, Julian's approach to food is as simplistic as the classic Italian dishes he loves. "I love food so much that it's part of everything I do. I love cooking for family and friends. I love that I know how to do it and it's not a chore. If you invite me over to your house, there's one room where you can always find me! Hopefully by the time people read this I will have my very own Italian restaurant opened. I always want to be able to do something with food that brings people together. It makes me so happy to see a room full of laughter and happiness from great food and of course great wine!"

Italian Wedding Soup | *"aka The Best Meatball Soup EVER!"*

1 onion, chopped

1 celery stalk, chopped

3 carrots, cut into rounds

2 garlic cloves, smashed

1 large head escarole, chopped

Olive oil

10–12 cups broth (depends on how much room there is in the pot)

MEATBALLS

1 clove garlic, smashed and chopped

¼ onion, diced

olive oil

1 tsp. oregano

1 tsp. parsley

1 tsp. sage

Milk or heavy cream (enough to moisten or soften the breadcrumbs and bread)

½ cup breadcrumbs or stale white bread

salt and pepper, to taste

1 lb. chopped meat

1 egg, beaten

½ cup Parmesan cheese

DIRECTIONS

SOUP

1. Sauté onions, celery, carrots, and garlic with 3 tablespoons olive oil to release flavors.

2. Add escarole and coat with oil.

3. Add broth. If you don't have enough, use water.

4. Add meatballs and their juices (recipe follows).

5. Slowly simmer for about an hour.

MEATBALL

1. Sauté garlic and onion with a little olive oil. Do not brown. When finished, add the herbs to the warm garlic and onions. Remove from heat and let cool.

2. Take bread and put in a bowl. Mix with heavy cream, using a little at a time. You don't want it in a puddle. Just enough to moisten it.

3. Add salt and pepper to breadcrumbs.

4. When onion mix is cooled, add to bread mixture and mix.

5. Preheat oven to 450 degrees. In a bigger bowl, add meat and egg. Use a fork to mix together properly.

6. Add bread mixture and cheese, and continue blending flavors with a fork, nice and even.

7. Shape meatballs with a tablespoon for consistent size. Make sure you keep moistening your hands in cold water while you roll them into proper balls. You will need to rinse your hands several times. When rolled into a ball, place them on a sheet pan and add ¼ inch water.

8. Cook until there's a nice brown color all around. When they are finished, you will add them and the water to the soup pot (you might have to add water to the pan if it dries out).

(l to r) Juliette, Natalia, Margaret, Julian

SHELLON & SHEVON JOHNSON
BROWNSVILLE, BROOKLYN

{ *Guyanese* }

Sisters Shellon and Shevon Johnson grew up in Brownsville, Brooklyn, in a home rich with the West Indian flavors of Guyana. "We were born in Queens, but moved to the Brownsville section of Brooklyn twenty-three years ago. Our parents were born and raised in Guyana, South America," says Shellon. Even though Brownsville is only about 1.6 square miles, it packs in some delicious worldly eats and Shellon loves being a part of that food landscape. "One thing about food, besides the fact that I cannot stop eating, is that I love to cook it. Trying new recipes and indulging in a new meal is something that I have enjoyed doing since I was a small child. I am most calm and comfortable when I cook and I oftentimes cook best when I am upset or feeling a little down. I just love food."

Brownsville's diversity is made up of people from around the globe: Jamaican, Puerto Rican, Italian, Chinese, Jewish, Trinidadian, Guyanese, Dominican, Haitian, and more. Shellon says of her own block, "I cannot speak for the whole of Brownsville, but the majority of our block consists of first and second generation West Indians. We are a very close-knit community and always look out for each other. " Shellon's tight-knit community is like most other communities: food is often the centerpiece—it's the "soul" that brings the people together. "The summertime is the best time to be in Brownsville because the whole community comes together. The children play with each other while the neighbors barbecue and play music that we all can enjoy. It's kind of like an unofficial block party," Shellon says with a reminiscent smile on her face. "During the holidays, you can always smell someone else's cooking: fried fish, fried plantains, jerk chicken. . . . You can almost always smell the scent of fresh baked bread from the Palagonia Italian Bread factory on Junius Avenue," just a short walk from Shellon and Shevon's home.

Shellon and Shevon Johnson

If there's one thing Shellon and Shevon could share with the world, it would be their mom's recipe for curry chicken. Shellon recalls learning the recipe from her mother. "She taught us at a very young age. By the time we were preteens we had already perfected the dish." Shellon and Shevon work together in the kitchen with complete synchronicity. One finishes what the other started without question or concern in the process of the recipe. There's no need; it's one they have made hundreds of times together before. What's most important to them in the kitchen is the togetherness, shown in their laughter, heard in their conversation, and finally expressed by the delicious flavors in the food that's shared with their family, community, and now, us.

Curry Chicken with White Rice

"Today, we decided to prepare curry chicken served with white rice. Although it originated in India, curry chicken is a dish that is prepared in Guyana by everyone, not just the Guyanese Indians. As children, we recall getting so excited every time we smelled the sweet aroma of curry. We loved the dish so much that one day our Mom decided it was time for us to learn how to make it. A great time to prepare this dish is literally any time you are in the mood for a nice, hearty meal. Curry chicken can be served with rice or roti at any time of year. It's a dish that's sure to satisfy your taste buds." — Shellon

3 lbs. chicken parts

1 lemon squeezed or ¼ cup vinegar

⅓ cup fresh herbs: thyme, basil, and oregano

1 tsp. vegetable oil

3 Tbsp. curry powder, separated

½ white onion, chopped

5 garlic cloves, minced

1 (15.5-oz.) can of channa (also known as garbanzo beans or chick peas)

3 medium-sized potatoes, quartered

4 cups water

Salt and pepper to taste

DIRECTIONS

1. Remove skin and excess fat from the chicken.

2. In a bowl, soak chicken in vinegar or lemon juice for 15 minutes.

3. Rub fresh herbs on the chicken.

4. Heat vegetable oil over medium heat in a nonstick pan.

5. Once heated, add 2 tablespoons of curry powder and allow to cook for 1 minute.

6. Add onions, garlic, chicken, and channa to the pan, and stir until chicken is fully coated with curry powder.

7. Cover and cook over medium heat for 15 minutes or until chicken is cooked.

8. Add water according to your desired amount of gravy.

9. Add 1 tablespoon of curry powder.

10. Increase heat to high. Add potatoes and stir until the pot begins to boil (*note: make sure the water covers the potatoes).

11. Add salt and pepper to taste.

12. Once the potatoes are soft, turn off your stove.

13. Serve over white rice or with rice on the side and enjoy!

NEW
YORK

JASON JAMAL NAKLEH
BAY RIDGE, BROOKLYN

{ *Seafood* }

We met Jason in Bay Ridge, Brooklyn, on a cloudy winter day. The Verrazano-Narrows Bridge was looming in the backdrop over the New York Bay, a beautiful and powerful sight. "I was born in 1974 in Manhattan and lived there until about 1976 when my parents moved us to Bay Ridge. I have been here ever since, except for a few years when I lived in Albany to go to college. My dad is originally from Palestine. He was born there in 1948 and moved here in 1970. My mom was half-Lebanese and half-Syrian and born and raised here in Bay Ridge Brooklyn. So I'm 100 percent Middle Eastern, but born and raised in the USA," Jason tells us, clarifying his immediate family's history for us.

Jason's family is like many in the Bay Ridge neighborhood of Brooklyn. It's not uncommon to find third or even fourth generation families living here. "My whole family has been here since the 1940s. My grandmother moved here in 1945, after living in Atlantic City and working at a shop on the boardwalk. She met my grandfather and they married in 1947. My mom was born in 1948, and she passed away from breast cancer in 1988 when I was thirteen," Jason says.

"Bay Ridge is originally Norwegian and Italian, but over the past thirty years, it's evolved into a true multicultural neighborhood. We've got everyone: Italian, Irish, Chinese, Middle Eastern, Norwegian, Greek, Mexican, and everything in between. You could walk a span of ten blocks and find a restaurant from each ethnicity I just mentioned. I believe Bay Ridge has the most restaurants and bars per block of any neighborhood in New York City. On 3rd avenue and 5th avenue especially, from 65th street to 101st street, there are several restaurants on every block."

Jason has many fond memories of growing up in Bay Ridge, most of them overflowing with flavorful food. "I spent a lot of time at my grandmother's house in Brooklyn as a child [my mother's

Jason Jamal and Tricia Ann Nakleh

side]. It was 'headquarters' for the family. We spent almost every major holiday there, with lots of food, everyone cooking, everyone nibbling. One Christmas somewhere around 1986, we were having a leg of lamb, and my uncle Bob was in charge of getting it in and out of the oven, and carving it. Somewhere along the line during cooking, the entire leg of lamb set ablaze inside the oven, like a huge fireball. The smoke alarms were going off, kids were running around, the women were screaming, and the fire wasn't going out. I quickly opened the kitchen window, and Uncle Bob proceeded to throw the entire leg of lamb out the window into the twelve inches of snow in the driveway, which quickly put the fire out. After a bit of cooling off and a bit of scraping off the charred bits, we still ate it, and from what I remember, it was still delicious!"

Today Jason and his wife have started some of their own food traditions, but Jason still incorporates subtle hints of his family's methodology into his cooking. One example is putting time and love into a dish. "I usually make it on a Sunday afternoon, and eat it for dinner on Sunday evening. I make enough for four servings, so my wife and I have it again on Monday night and we don't have to cook after a long day of work. It tastes even better the second day, once all of the flavors have had a chance to get to know each other," Jason says, smiling. In all seriousness, Jason says, "When I make this chili to enter in a chili cook-off, I usually make it the night ahead so the flavors meld. I've entered two chili cook-offs, and have won both times with this recipe! I believe it's truly an original."

Just like this dish, Jason is a truly original character. He works as a professional photographer by day and a burgeoning chef by night. He sums up the two perfectly by saying, "I'm not afraid to get my hands dirty, I'm not afraid to try something new, and I'm always on the hunt for interesting, exciting flavors!"

Award-Winning Seafood Chili Recipe

"Today I made my twice-award-winning 'Seafood Chili.' It's a recipe I came up with myself, and after a few failed attempts, I finally got it right. It came about because my wife doesn't eat any red meat or pork, only chicken and seafood. I had never seen or heard of a seafood chili before, so I came up with one myself! It doesn't have any greasiness that regular chili has, and it's super healthy—only two tablespoons of olive oil for four servings, and only fresh, clean ingredients!" — *Jason Jamal Nakleh*

2 Tbsp. extra virgin olive oil

2 medium onions, chopped

2 medium shallots, chopped

4 garlic cloves, chopped

4 anchovies, chopped

1 tsp. salt, more to taste

2 tsp. dried oregano

2 tsp. dried thyme

2 tsp. chili powder

1 tsp. chipotle chili powder

1 tsp. smoked paprika

2 Tbsp. tomato paste

1 (12-oz.) dark beer, room temperature

1½ tsp. instant coffee

1 (28-oz.) can whole peeled tomatoes (preferably Italian, San Marzano)

1 (19-oz.) can white or red kidney beans, (use 2 cans if you like more beans)

½ cup water

1 (8-oz.) bottle clam juice

2 Tbsp. honey

1 tsp. ground pepper

½ tsp. crushed red pepper, more to taste

¼ tsp. cayenne pepper, more to taste

1½ to 2 lbs. of a mix of the following seafood, cut into bite-sized pieces: shrimp, snow crab, lobster tail, and scallops.

TOPPINGS

white rice

sour cream

shredded cheddar cheese

chives

tortilla chips

DIRECTIONS

1. In a 5-quart high walled stock pot, heat the olive oil on medium heat until shimmering.

2. Add the onions and shallots and cook over medium heat for about 10 minutes until they are caramelized.

3. Add the garlic and the anchovies. Using a wooden spoon, break up the anchovies so they melt into the aromatics, about 2 minutes. NOTE: The anchovies are important! They will make the chili taste of the sea.

4. Add the salt, oregano, thyme, chili powder, chipotle powder, and smoked paprika. Stir so the spices mix with the aromatics into a gel-like consistency. NOTE: Make sure to use smoked paprika. Regular paprika has a different taste. The smoked paprika tastes like barbecue potato chips and is smoky and sweet.

5. Add the tomato paste and stir well. Let the mixture cook for a minute or two.

6. Add the beer and stir. Use your wooden spoon to scrape up all the brown bits from the bottom of the pot.

7. Add the coffee and stir to incorporate. Let the mixture simmer and reduce by half. This takes about 8 minutes. NOTE: Coffee is important because it gives the chili a rounded, earthy taste.

8. While the mixture is simmering, put the beans in a colander. Rinse and drain them. Set aside.

9. Take the tomatoes (with their liquid) and put them into a large bowl. Use your hands to break up the whole tomatoes into little chunks. It should be a chunky consistency.

10. After the mixture has reduced, add the tomatoes and the beans. Stir to incorporate fully. Add the ½ cup of water now as well. Stir everything well.

11. Add the clam juice and the honey. Add the black pepper, crushed red pepper, and cayenne pepper as well. You can add more pepper if you like it spicier.

12. Reduce the heat to low and cover. Simmer gently for about a half hour. NOTE: Simmer it on really low heat for as long as you like, really. The longer you simmer it, the better it will taste.

13. If you are using crab, you can add the crab while it is simmering to flavor the sauce. If you are using shrimp, lobster, or scallops, wait a little bit and let the chili simmer.

14. After it has simmered for about a half hour, uncover and check the consistency. If it's too thick, add a little water. If it's too thin, let it simmer uncovered for a little while and reduce the sauce.

15. Add the remainder of the seafood about 10 minutes before you are ready to serve. If the seafood is cut into bite-sized pieces, it will only take several minutes to cook in the simmering pot. Add the seafood, stir to incorporate, and cook for 5–10 minutes until cooked through. Be sure to not overcook the seafood. It will continue to cook in the hot chili while it's resting.

16. Serve the chili over white rice, with a dollop of sour cream and other toppings you like. Enjoy!

RENIA WILLIAMS & ROBIN WALLACE
CANARSIE, BROOKLYN

{ *Southern* }

New York City is full of transplants. Renia and her family know this very well: "Although I live in New York, I'm an implant from South Carolina. My father's family moved here during the 'great migration' when black families left the 'Jim Crow' south for a better way of life. My mother's family remained in the South. During the summers we would come visit in Brooklyn. When we finished high school, one by one, we moved to Brooklyn. Some of my father's family has returned to the South in their retirement years, but only a few. After I moved to New York, I only lived here for a little over one year before I joined the military. I wasn't planning on making a career out of it, but I did. After I retired from the Navy, I stayed in Virginia for five years and then went to North Carolina for two. After North Carolina, I decide to come back to Brooklyn in 2010."

So in a way, Renia moved in and out of New York City and today calls Brooklyn home again. She lives with her older sister Robin in the Canarsie neighborhood of Brooklyn, which she describes: "It's mostly an island community filled with folks from various Caribbean Islands. There's a few Jewish families as well as a few Latinos. I'm actually learning to tell the difference in which island people are from based on their accents. During the summer, on almost every block, all you smell is various types of barbecue. You see people outside playing dominos and the children riding their bikes. The neighborhood is friendly and inviting, for the most part. I've tried several different foods since becoming close friends with my neighbors."

Renia and her sister still hold tight to many of the Southern dishes they had growing up. "We both cook traditional Southern food, and we also try out new recipes. During the week we don't cook a

Renia Williams

meal every day—we just throw something together quick and easy—but on Sunday I normally cook the traditional Sunday dinner for my sister, her best friend, and myself, and there is always enough if someone were to drop by. There's an open invitation for Sunday dinner."

Growing up in South Carolina, Renia learned how to cook from her grandmother. "I always loved food and watching my grandmother cook. I would watch her in the kitchen and sometimes she would let me help. As we got older, we were allowed to cook, but only on Saturdays, and it would be something simple like hotdogs and hamburgers." It wasn't until they got much older that Renia and her sister were able to pitch in for Sunday supper duties.

Sunday dinners were a big deal in Renia's family. "Sunday dinner was like a mini family reunion. It really didn't matter what was cooked, it was always delicious. Everyone went to church and after church family members you didn't see on a regular basis during the week came by Granny's house for Sunday dinner. This is the reason we do a traditional Sunday dinner today. When I go visit my mother in South Carolina, it's the same—everyone comes over for Sunday dinner."

Being in the kitchen helping her grandmother cook was one of Renia's fondest memories as a child, along with her grandmother's "homemade pancakes from scratch on Saturday mornings with sausages." Renia had plenty of favorites from her grandmother's recipe bank: "My favorite dishes from my grandmother were her sweet potato pie and homemade yeast biscuits. I wished someone had written the recipes down. I have yet to taste anything close to hers. I have found various recipes and tried them, but so far, nothing can compare to my Granny's."

Renia continues to reflect on her Granny's, this time with a sense of sadness: "It's important to remember signature dishes from your family members. Write them down. That way you can pass them on to the next generation. That's one of my regrets: not writing down some of my Granny's recipes, especially her yeast biscuits and sweet potato pies." While those recipes may have been taken to the grave with Granny, her memory is being passed on right here in the pages of this book. It's that spirit, that soul, which Renia is putting into her food today that's important.

Fried Spareribs

"The two recipes I've put together are my grandmother's baked macaroni and cheese (I've changed it a little for my taste in food) and fried ribs that I tasted at the state fair in Alabama in 1999. It's basically the same concept as frying chicken but using ribs instead. These dishes can be cooked anytime and can be used as the main course for Sunday dinner." — Renia

1 package of pork baby back ribs, sliced individually (normally 6 to 9 ribs)

DRY RUB FOR RIBS

1 Tbsp. garlic salt

1 Tbsp. ground cumin

1 Tbsp. paprika

2 Tbsp. black pepper, separated

1 Tbsp. onion powder

1 cup flour

2 cups canola oil

DIRECTIONS

1. Mix all dry ingredients except for 1 tablespoon black pepper, onion powder, and flour. Season the ribs with this mixture.

2. Place flour into large ziplock plastic bag and add 1 tablespoon of black pepper and onion powder. Shake to mix well and set aside.

3. Pour oil into cast iron frying pan. Turn on medium heat.

4. Massage dry rub into ribs one final time.

5. Put ribs into flour mix and shake.

6. Place ribs into frying pan and cook on one side for about 10 minutes. Check for desired brownness and turn over. Note: Depending on the thickness of ribs, cook time will vary.

7. Once ribs are cooked, drain on paper towels and serve.

Robin Wallace

Baked Mac & Cheese

4 cups elbow macaroni

8 oz. Colby Jack cheese

8 oz. whole milk mozzarella
  cheese

8 oz. mild cheddar cheese

1 can cream of chicken soup

¾ soup can of milk

paprika to taste

black pepper to taste

1 stick real butter

DIRECTIONS

1. Boil noodles as directed, but do not cook them completely.

2. Grate cheeses and mix them together in a large bowl.

3. Preheat oven to 350 degrees.

4. In a 9 x 13 nonstick baking dish, layer noodles and then cheese. Repeat twice, leaving about half a cup of cheese. Place extra cheese to the side.

5. Empty can of soup into a pot. Fill ¾ of soup can with milk and add to pot.

6. Using a whisk, stir milk and soup together over low heat.

7. Once mixture is smooth, remove from heat and pour over layered macaroni and cheese.

8. Place small slices of butter on top of macaroni and cheese.

9. Bake in oven for 20–30 minutes.

10. Remove from oven and stir. Place remaining cheese on top and sprinkle with black pepper and paprika.

11. Bake for another 10 minutes or until top cheese is melted and golden.

Cabbage Salad

1 small head of cabbage   *⅓ cup mayonnaise*   *2 Tbsp. sugar*

1 cup fresh salsa   *1 Tbsp. pepper*   *2 Tbsp. white vinegar*

DIRECTIONS

1. Chop cabbage and place in a bowl.

2. Combine remaining ingredients and mix well.

3. Chill in your refrigerator before serving.

JOEY GLOVER

COBBLE HILL, BROOKLYN

{ *Japanese* }

Joey is new to the whole "cooking thing," but he has learned a lot in the past several years . . . he's had to. Having a wife from Japan and being a work-from-home dad, he's had to at least learn the basics to feed his family. "I made mahimahi, miso soup, and Japanese brown rice. My mother-in-law taught me a couple different variations of this recipe, so I've modified a few things, like I use this steam oven but my mother-in-law will usually bake it [the fish] sitting inside the sauce. Hers is better than mine," Joey says, laughing. "[She taught me] mainly just the basics of how to use the ingredients that are usually used in Japanese cooking."

Joey and his wife have very different cultural backgrounds and have never purposely created any family dishes that fuse their two backgrounds together. But that doesn't mean the two worlds don't meet up in the kitchen every now and then. "I'm originally from Indialantic, Florida—my mom's from Alabama, and my pop's is a full-blown Florida cracker. My wife is from Kitakyushu, Japan. We never really consciously do any fusion, but my American hand always seems to do something a little different. We take trips to Florida and Alabama, and my wife loves southern food. When she was pregnant, we visited my grandmother in Alabama, and my wife gained major weight. Eating southern food in New York is just never the same. My grandmother always says, 'They put sugar in their corn bread.'"

When it comes down to his reason for cooking, Joey keeps it simple: "I mainly cook so I can feed my boy and wife good healthy stuff. I like to try and impress my wife. Recently I started cooking clams. I had never made them before, but my wife seems to really like them. That makes me happy."

Ayumi Yamamoto, Joey Glover, Godai

Food has always been a universal language, and Joey is starting to realize this now more than ever. "Culture and food say a lot about people. In most cultures, food and eating seems to be the time everyone spends together. This is especially true in Japan; food is everything, food is always a party . . . and it's always delicious."

Steamed Fish

"The original dish is called 'nitsuke,' which means boiled fish. She (my mother-in-law) taught me to make it by boiling it in a pan or skillet. I have changed it to steam broil, so I'm not sure if this still really counts as 'nitsuke' but it uses the same marinade." — Joey

FISH (today I used mahimahi)

12 oz. fish

¼ cup mirin

¼ cup sake

¼ cup sweetener (maple syrup, agave, or honey)

¼ cup purified water

¼ cup soy sauce

DIRECTIONS

1. Mix all of your ingredients, and let fish marinate for about 15 minutes.

2. Preheat oven to 425 degrees. Place the fish on a piece of foil and pour ⅛ tablespoon of marinade and other desired flavors onto the foil. Wrap the fish entirely with foil.

3. Place fish into oven for 15 minutes. This process is known as "bake steaming."

4. Broil fish for an additional 15 minutes.

Miso Soup

This recipe for miso soup makes about 8 servings

8 cups cold tap water

1 pint mushrooms

1 small carrot, peeled and shredded

1½ tsp. instant dashi (broth)

½ cup cubed tofu

1 bunch of kale

1 bunch of broccoli

¼ cup miso paste

DIRECTIONS

1. Pour the tap water into a pot along with the mushrooms and carrots and bring to a boil.

2. Add the instant dashi and whisk to dissolve.

3. Turn the heat to medium-low and add the tofu, kale, and broccoli. Simmer for 2 minutes.

4. In the meantime, put the miso paste into a bowl. Ladle about ½ cup of the hot dashi broth into the bowl and whisk to melt the miso paste so that the mixture is smooth.

5. Turn the heat off, add the miso paste mixture to the pot, and stir well.

6. If the soup needs more flavor, add an additional tablespoon or two of miso paste or soy sauce, to taste.

NIMAI LARSON

BEDFORD-STUYVESANT, BROOKLYN

{ *Vegetarian BBQ* }

Nimai, like many Brooklynites, transplanted to King's County from elsewhere—in her case, she migrated from Texas. The artistic vibe, sense of community, and amazing diversity of the people and food and music were just a few of the things that drew her, like many, to Brooklyn. She specifically calls the neighborhood of Bedford-Stuyvesant home, a neighborhood in transition.

The well-known neighborhood slogan "Bed-Stuy: Do or Die" might still exist, but the context is very different than it was a decade ago because the neighborhood is experiencing a massive gentrification. Because of this, Nimai has noticed a drastic change in the food landscape. "In Bed-Stuy, we have a rapidly changing food scene because of recent high-impact gentrification. When my sister and I moved here in 2010, the normal food fare ranged from authentic Soul Food, to Afro-Caribbean, to a lot of Trinidadian Doubles shops. The Doubles, fried flat bread with curried chickpeas inside, were to die for! We'd get ours from a spot on Fulton Street and then walk over to Charlie's Calypso Record shop to listen to Soca music. Everyone we talked to on the street had a friendly disposition, always wished us a good day, and complimented us on our wacky fashion and bright smiles. Walking down Bedford Avenue on any given summer day in Bed-Stuy, we would walk past the fragrant smoke of a Grill 'n' Chill party or a church BBQ fund-raiser. The grill masters would always have a smile on their faces, and why shouldn't they? They are providing the best service to their friends and family by preparing them food!

"Around 2013, my sister and I discovered four new coffee shops within walking distance from us. One of them carries Dough Doughnuts, which is a Bed-Stuy based gourmet doughnut shop. It's a little piece of paradise. . . . We also met some of the people who work at Speedy Romeos, a classy

wood-fired pizza spot down the street that is also utilized for the set of the HBO show *Girls*. Slowly but surely, new bakeries offering gluten-free and vegan muffins, fresh markets carrying locally grown produce, taco joints with sizzling potato and poblano specials, and gourmet restaurants serving the finest Italian fare have been establishing themselves in Bed-Stuy. So have many, many more people who have wacky fashion! Our neighborhood has become a melting pot in its truest sense; there are people and food from all over the world and all walks of life coexisting together. I have mega Bed-Stuy pride!"

Do or Die!

Nimai's creative energy and varied culinary tastes originate from her own diverse background. "Originally, my dad's side of the family is from Sweden and my mom's side is Russian Jewish. I hear I have relatives on my mom's side that live in the Williamsburg area of Brooklyn. . . . I need to do some further investigation!" Her recipe in this book pays homage to her upbringing in Texas. "My inspiration came from combining my laid-back, southern comfort surroundings as a child in Texas with my now classy, high-maintenance foodie surroundings as an adult in New York.

"I was raised vegetarian in Texas—the BBQ capital of the world. While most people would see this as a tragedy or comedy of errors, I saw it as a beautiful challenge—an opportunity to make the healthiest, freshest vegetarian food taste like the juiciest, most traditional, meaty, southern comfort food."

Her love of cooking was also instilled in her at an early age by her family. "It has always felt very natural for me to provide for and nurture those around me . . . what better way than to cook for them!"

Music is also a driving and powerful force in Nimai's life. Touring the world playing music has also contributed to her diverse palette. She has toured the world with her band, Prince Rama, and has shared meals with people around the world. She quickly learned that both food and music are a universal language, a way to connect with others.

Her band, Prince Rama, has been playing music together since they were in high school and professionally for the past six years. "Our music is loud, dancey, and fun! My sister, Taraka, plays guitar and sings. Our soul-sister, Sasha Lord, plays keyboards and sampler. And I play the drums and sing. It's been a blessing making a career out of creating music, traveling, and performing. Prince Rama has allowed us to circle the globe several times! Some of our favorite spots are Brazil, Colombia, Estonia, Russia, Turkey, Slovenia, Tasmania, Australia, and Portugal."

For Nimai, "Music is a form of community bonding; a universal language if you will. Everywhere we have traveled, music has been the gel holding this world together. Listening to music is something we all have in common, whether it's hip-hop, classical, jazz, bluegrass, witch house, trance, psychedelic, garage rock, or Thai pop. It helps us get through the day. Similarly, food is also a common thread that is woven through the world, binding us together."

These days, Nimai is just as passionate about music as she is food. "I keep an online cookbook called 'Nimai's Cookbook' that can be found online at www.nimailarson.com. Our band, Prince Rama, can be found online too or by visiting www.princerama.com! Who knows, a cooking demonstration/live show could be coming to a city near you!" That would be amazing!

Corn Muffins

"Today I made Sauteed Tofu planks with Cranberry-Chipotle BBQ sauce topped with a Purple Cabbage and Radish kraut, Honey-Roasted Brussel Sprouts, and Gluten-Free Corn Muffins. A good time is anytime you are looking to impress—whether it's a romantic date, a family dinner, new friends, or the in-laws. Look no further! The tofu is rich in protein and the sauce is bold and spicy. The brussels are sweet, tender, and naturally provide lots of Vitamin C. The corn muffins are moist, nurturing, and do not leave you feeling heavy. This is true southern comfort food in a healthy disguise! Everything is gluten-free and the tofu and brussels sprouts are dairy-free. The trick to changing your diet is taking the dishes that are 'guilty pleasures' and turning them into 'guiltless pleasures.'" — *Nimai*

2 cups gluten-free flour

¾ cup corn meal

2 tsp. salt

1 tsp. baking soda

1 cup brown sugar

1 cup organic whole milk

¾ cup organic buttermilk

3 Tbsp. corn

2 Tbsp. whole milk ricotta

1 tsp. apple cider vinegar

DIRECTIONS

1. Preheat oven to 350 degrees

2. Combine the gluten-free flour, corn meal, salt, and baking soda in a small bowl. In a larger bowl, combine the rest of the ingredients.

3. Slowly incorporate the dry ingredients into the wet ingredients while using an electric beater on its lowest setting. Be careful not to overmix; 10–14 seconds is enough.

4. In two greased 12-cup muffin trays, spoon enough batter into each cup to fill it about ¾ full. Bake for 7 minutes, rotate the trays, then bake for another 7 minutes. When the full 14 minutes are up, remove the muffins from their trays immediately so the heat does not keep baking them, this will cause them to dry out.

5. Serve with butter, honey, or your favorite jam.

Tofu Planks

1 (16-oz.) pkg. extra firm tofu

2 cups nutritional yeast (also known as "brewer's yeast")

olive oil

DIRECTIONS

1. Drain, rinse, and then dry the tofu block. Cut into 6 planks. Coat the top side of each plank with nutritional yeast.

2. Generously pour olive oil into a nonstick pan on medium heat. Carefully place the 6 planks, nutritional yeast side facing down, into the pan. Coat the top side of the planks with the remainder of the nutritional yeast and let the tofu cook.

3. After about 8 minutes, check to see if the bottom side is brown and crispy. If it is, flip it. Let the other side get brown and crispy the same way and remove from heat.

4. Serve with Nimai's Cranberry-Chipotle BBQ Sauce and Purple Cabbage and Radish Kraut (recipes below).

Nimai's Cranberry-Chipotle BBQ Sauce

1 cup roasted red peppers

¾ cup dried cranberries

3 chipotle peppers in Adobo sauce

2 garlic cloves

1 Tbsp. chopped ginger

2 tsp. brown sugar

2 tsp. olive oil

DIRECTIONS

1. Roughly chop all ingredients except brown sugar and olive oil and place into a food processor.

2. Add the brown sugar and olive oil and blend until smooth.

Purple Cabbage and Radish Kraut

1 cup chopped purple cabbage

1 cup sliced radish

1 Tbsp. chopped fresh cilantro

Juice from half of a fresh lime

1 tsp. black sesame seeds

1 tsp. apple cider vinegar

1 tsp. olive oil

DIRECTIONS

1. Combine purple cabbage, radish, and cilantro in a small bowl. Add the lime juice, black sesame seeds, apple cider vinegar, and olive oil. Toss all of the ingredients together well and serve!

Honey-Roasted Brussels Sprouts

20–25 brussels sprouts

½ cup honey

olive oil

salt, black pepper, crushed red pepper flakes to taste

DIRECTIONS

1. Rinse the brussels sprouts and drain. On a cutting board, cut off the ends and chop each brussels sprout in half. Throw away the ends.

2. Generously coat the bottom of a cast-iron skillet with olive oil. Add salt, black pepper, and crushed red pepper flakes to taste.

3. Lay down each brussels sprout half, face down, starting with the outer edges of your skillet and making your way in towards the center. When all of the brussels sprouts have been placed, turn the heat on low. Cover and let cook undisturbed for about 20 minutes or until the bottoms are browned and crispy.

4. Turn off the heat and drizzle the honey evenly over the tops. Replace the cover for 1–2 minutes. Serve and enjoy!

RENE ABDO AND SON

BUSHWICK, BROOKLYN

{ *Jamaican* }

Rene and her son live in the vibrant and energetic neighborhood of Bushwick, Brooklyn. Bushwick is another Brooklyn neighborhood that is quickly being gentrified and has become a more heterogeneous community. "Our neighborhood in Brooklyn is currently in transition," Rene says. "There is a lot of development and rebuilding of properties. It's pretty quiet during the cold months but during the warm months, it's almost a party in the streets every weekend. Everyone is playing music out of the windows, out of the cars, on the bicycle boom box, just everywhere! Lots of BBQs on the rooftops and sidewalks. The demographics of this neighborhood are highly Latin from the Caribbean but changing to be a true melting pot." Bushwick is bordered by Ridgewood, Queens, and the other legendary Brooklyn neighborhoods: Williamsburg, East New York, Brownsville, Highland Park, and Bedford-Stuyvesant. It's no wonder that Bushwick has become an energetic hotbed for art, culture, and, most importantly, food.

Rene brings this neighborhood energy and vibrancy into her kitchen through a traditional Jamaican dish that her aunt taught her how to make. "I made Escovitch Fish and Festivals." Festival is a fried-dumpling-like dough that is sweet and crispy on the outside and dense in the middle. "I watched my aunt Holly make it and that's how I learned. This recipe is special to my family . . . it is our fast food. Fast Jamaican food always brings good times and good laughs among friends and family. It's special to me because it reminds me of the pristine beaches we used to visit as kids and this dish was the best part of a beach day! Eating with sand on your hands, sun everywhere . . . it was always amazing."

Rene and King Abdo

Escovitch Fish and Festivals are a Jamaican staple on the weekends. The best part about it is that the longer the fish soaks in the vinegar, the better it tastes.

Preserving this dish and teaching it to her son is incredibly important to Rene. "It's very important to save family dishes to save your culture," she says. If they are forgotten, "everything that makes your family come together for special moments created over meals will be lost. Tradition is important and teaching children where they are from is important to maintain our individuality." This dish provides Rene and her son an undeniable sense of pride, culture, home, and the rebirth of these feelings from one generation to the next. Share in this celebration with them and try this dish at home.

Escovitch Fish

"Food to me is the center of everything! I love food, I love to cook, and I love to eat healthy, tasty, fresh food. I often do huge dinner parties for my friends and always run out of food because they like it so much." — Rene

1 red snapper, about 2 lbs.

1 lime

vegetable oil for frying, about 1 cup

1 scallion, chopped

1 small onion, sliced

2 carrots, julienned

½ bell pepper, sliced

handful of pimento seeds (Allspice)

1½ cup vinegar

¼ tsp. salt

¼ tsp. black pepper

DIRECTIONS

1. Clean and trim your fish. Then squeeze the juice of the lime over it. Massage the juice into the fish, rinse with cool water, and then pat dry.

2. Season it with salt and pepper, to taste.

3. Using a sharp knife, cut slits across the belly of the fish on both sides. This will allow for faster cooking and help the salt and black pepper as well as the escovitch sauce to really infuse the fish.

4. Heat the vegetable oil on medium, and then gently add the seasoned fish to the pan. Allow this to cook for 4–5 minutes on each side or until you have a nice golden color and a crispy outside. You'll need tongs and a fork or spoon to flip the fish.

5. In a saucepan add the rest of the ingredients to make the sauce. Place saucepan on medium heat and bring to a gentle simmer. Allow this to simmer for 3–5 minutes until the onion and bell pepper are slightly tender.

Festivals

2 cups self-rising flour

1 cup cornmeal

2 tsp. salt

½ cup soft brown sugar

1 egg

1 tsp. vanilla extract

1 cup vegetable oil

Water as needed

DIRECTIONS

1. Add all the dry ingredients into a bowl and mix well.

2. In a separate bowl, mix egg and vanilla, and set aside.

3. Fold egg and vanilla mixture into the dry ingredients. Then slowly add water and knead dough to a thick batter consistency.

4. Portion out finger-long dumplings (measure your middle finger joint to the end of your palm where it meets your wrist).

5. Set aside for 10 minutes and let rest.

6. Fry the dumplings on medium heat until golden brown on all sides, flipping occasionally.

7. Remove from oil and place dumplings on a paper towel–lined plate to cool.

8. Place fish on a plate and pour sauce over very liberally. Dress with onions, peppers, and carrots. Serve along with festival for maximum deliciousness!

PATTY

CANARSIE, BROOKLYN

{ *Haitian* }

We visited Patty on a special evening of fun and food at her home in Canarsie, Brooklyn. She was having a dinner party with her sister and some friends and made some traditional Haitian recipes to share with not only her guests, but also with us in this book.

It was a night of traditional Haitian recipes she learned how to make from her mother: "My mother taught me how to cook, which is typical in the Haitian culture. We made purple potato salad, black rice with crab and shrimp, and beans and rice. Typical Haitian cuisine has a lot of spices, herbs, and vegetables. All this is to give the food more flavor and it helps build your immune system."

Patty's family comes from both the city and the country regions of Haiti which have different influences on her cooking, "My family is from Haiti. My mother is from Port-au-Prince (Haiti's capital) and my dad is from Petit-Goâve (the country side). The fondest food memory for me was fried plantains and meatballs and rice. My mother would use the meatballs to substitute for regular meat to mix with the rice. The fried plantains were actually made as a form of homemade chip since plantains are more grown and used on the island."

Like most Brooklynites, Patty and her sister have "found home where the heart is," well in this case more like "found home where the stomach is." They live in a neighborhood in Brooklyn with many different Caribbean people, including other Haitians, "I live in Canarsie, which has now become more of a Caribbean neighborhood. There's a lot more Caribbean restaurants and markets that sell food, spices, and veggies straight from the island. During the summertime when Caribbeans cook the most with the front door open, you'll be able to walk down the street near a few homes and you'll

smell the aroma of spices or jerk chicken in the rotisserie which makes your tummy growl. The meal we made today definitely matches our neighborhood. Since my neighborhood is infused with Haitian and Jamaican culture, it's typical."

Having her sister with her in Brooklyn means a lot to Patty, especially when thinking about her family and the meals they shared together. These meals strike a chord of love, culture, and family within Patty that is deeply important to her, "Yes, our family does cook often. It's very important to pass down the tradition, it reminds our family how it important it is to stay together and never forget where we came from. Food to me means culture and memories. Food brings the most out of our Haitian tradition. I think [food is] important because it preserves our Haitian culture and reminds us of our ancestors. Also, it shows the new generation how things were done back then." A showing of great importance to us all.

Black Rice (Djon Djon)

2 cups djon-djon mushrooms

4 cups water

1 small onion, chopped

4 garlic cloves, minced

2 Tbsp. olive oil

2–3 sprigs of thyme

½ tsp. ground cloves

2 cups long grain rice (you can also use jasmine or basmati rice)

salt and pepper to taste

1 cup frozen lima beans

1 scotch bonnet pepper

*optional: 1 cube vegetable bouillon

DIRECTIONS

1. Bring mushrooms to a boil in water. Reduce heat to low and let steep for about 20 minutes.

2. Strain the mushrooms but keep the water, which will now be black. This water will be used to cook the rice in.

3. Saute the onion and garlic in the olive oil until they start to brown.

4. Stir in the thyme and cloves.

5. Add the rice while continuing to stir.

6. Add the water that was drained off from the boiled mushrooms.

7. Salt and pepper to taste. Note: add the bouillon cube here is desired.

8. Stir in the lima beans.

9. Bring mixture to a boil until the water begins to evaporate.

10. Lower the heat and place the whole scotch bonnet pepper on top of the rice. Cover tightly and allow to cook for about 20 minutes.

11. Check that the rice is cooked all the way through (not crunchy). Remove from heat and you are ready to serve.

Patty and Bernadine

Rice and Beans

¼ cup oil

¼ tsp. ground cloves

1¼ cups of white rice

a few leafs of parsley

3 sprigs thyme

1 can pink beans

3 cups water

salt and pepper to taste

DIRECTIONS

1. Place a medium-size pot on medium heat and add oil.

2. Add the cloves, rice, parsley, and thyme and toast 1–2 minutes. The rice should begin to become translucent.

3. Add the beans and water. Bring to a boil and stir. Then reduce to low heat.

4. Put lid on pot and let simmer 12–13 minutes, stirring occasionally.

5. Once the water is absorbed, remove from heat and let sit for 5 minutes.

Purple Potato Salad

2 Idaho potatoes

1 small beet

½ onion

2 leafs of parsley

½ cup mayo

1 tsp. olive oil

salt and pepper

DIRECTIONS

1. Peel potatoes and beet.

2. Cut potatoes and beet into cubes.

3. Cover potatoes and beet in a large pot of water. Boil until tender.

4. Chop the onions and the parsley until it's minced.

5. In a large bowl, mix potatoes and beet together with onions, parsley, and mayo. Mix well.

6. Add olive oil, and salt and pepper to taste.

QUEENS | NEW YORK

Considered to be one of the most ethnically diverse places on the planet, it's no wonder Queens has such a vast food landscape. It houses more than a quarter of New York City's population, and our guests from Queens represent Guyana, Puerto Rico, China, Poland, and the Philippines. Modern-day Queens is going back to the borough's earliest beginnings as farmland by currently hosting the largest urban rooftop farm in the city. It provides Queens residents with locally grown fruits and vegetables. With its enormous diversity and access to a great variety of fresh foods, Queens is a borough filled with deliciousness.

LIZ CRESPO SPEARS
KEW GARDENS, QUEENS

{ *Puerto Rican* }

New York City has some of the best food histories because of families like Liz Crespo Spears. Her New York story comes from a multigenerational family that started in Puerto Rico and came to New York in the 1930s. They not only have a deep family history in the city but also a deliciously rich food history.

These days Liz and her husband, Charles, call Kew Gardens, Queens, home. "My husband and I have lived here for thirteen years. It is very representative of the diversity that is Queens. You will find Eastern European groceries just blocks away from Latin American groceries. For dinner on any given night, I could walk to any number of restaurants—Italian, Latin American, Turkish, Chinese, Indian, Thai, West Indian, among others. The neighborhood is truly a melting pot!

"The typical Latin American market here is bustling with noise (both Spanish and English being spoken simultaneously and, most definitely, salsa music playing). It's overflowing with the flavors of Latin America like: plantains, banana leaves, mangos, coconuts, cilantro, peppers, yucca, beans, and many of the ingredients we use in this potato pie dish."

Liz continues her family's historical journey in New York. "My grandparents came to New York City from Puerto Rico in the 1930s. My dad and his seven siblings grew up on 110th Street in Manhattan's Spanish Harlem in the 1950s. Growing up, he had extended family living in the same tenement building. So many family traditions revolved around delicious food. Both of my dad's parents were amazing cooks, and he learned the best from them."

In 1957, Liz's family relocated to the Lower East Side of Manhattan to the Smith Houses. "I have aunts and uncles who still live there today and many holidays were celebrated there. In the 1960s,

my dad moved to the Bay Shore/Brentwood area on Long Island. That area is where many Puerto Ricans from NYC relocated, and it's where I grew up and lived until adulthood."

One dish from those many holidays spent on the Lower East Side was a dish called, "Potato Pie," a fusion of a traditional English Shepherd's Pie (the mashed potato part) and a Puerto Rican Shepherd's Pie called Pastelon that is made with plantains and Puerto Rican–style meat.

Liz's father, Frank, taught her how to cook from the early age of six. She vividly recalls, "I remember stirring oatmeal as it cooked, to keep it smooth and creamy, and learning to fry an egg. As I got older, my dad taught me many of his best recipes, and I have many memories of spending time together in the kitchen."

Liz takes the importance of passing down and documenting traditional family recipes very seriously. "Food feeds the body and the soul. It really is such a strong connection between the generations of a family. I tell my own children so many stories from my own childhood of our big family celebrations. Sharing these recipes with my boys is like giving them a window into our family history and allowing them to experience firsthand our rich culture." It's for these reasons I created *Real Food Real Kitchens*: family, food, culture, and history.

Frank Crespo's Potato Pie

"My dad created this recipe when I was a kid (more than thirty years ago), and it is still a family favorite. It is on the Thanksgiving table every year. Both my sister and I have learned how to cook it from watching my dad over the years, but he still advises us to make sure it comes out like his original recipe. I grew up with two brothers and two sisters and my dad now has eleven grandchildren and three great-grandchildren. This recipe has been the center of many good natured arguments when dividing up holiday leftovers. When I cook traditional Puerto Rican food, I feel connected to my past and especially to my dad. He passed on his story and memories through food. Whenever I'm in my kitchen cooking, I feel his presence beside me, guiding me." — Liz

Turkey Picadillo (bottom layer of pie)

1 lb. 94% lean ground turkey

½ medium onion, diced

½ medium red bell pepper, diced

4 garlic cloves, minced

3 Tbsp. chopped pimento

3 Tbsp. homemade or store-bought sofrito (see recipe below)

¼ cup pitted green olives

1½ tsp. Adobo

¾ tsp. black pepper

¾ tsp. dried oregano

1 tsp. salt

¼ tsp. crushed red pepper

1 (14.5-oz.) can petite cut tomatoes

2 cups water

DIRECTIONS

1. Brown turkey in large skillet.

2. Add onions, peppers, and garlic, and cook until onions are transparent.

3. Add remaining ingredients and cook on medium-low heat until sauce cooks down (approximately 1 hour).

Plantains (middle layer of pie)

2 ripe plantains (best when skin is almost completely black)   *Vegetable oil for frying*

DIRECTIONS

1. Peel and slice plantains on an angle (so they are elongated, not little perfect circles) into ½-inch thick slices.

2. Fry in oil until brown and edges get slightly crispy.

Mashed Potatoes (top layer of pie)

5 lb. potatoes   *1 cup heavy cream*

¾ cup grated Parmesan cheese   *½ stick salted butter*

1 cup milk   *Salt and black pepper, to taste*

DIRECTIONS

1. Peel and cut potatoes into 1-inch cubes.

2. In a large pot, cover potatoes with cold, salted water, and boil until soft (about 25 minutes).

3. Transfer potatoes to a large bowl, draining the water, and add Parmesan cheese.

4. Use masher to break chunks apart.

5. Heat milk, cream, and butter in small saucepan until butter melts (do not boil).

6. Add half of the milk mixture to the potatoes and beat with an electric hand mixer.

7. Continue slowly adding milk mixture until potatoes are smooth and creamy, but still stiff enough to maintain a shape. You may have leftover milk.

8. Add salt and pepper to taste.

(l to r) Jessica, Charlie, Owen, Frank (center back), Charles (front and center), Liz, Anna

Pie Assembly

2 store-bought deep dish pie crusts   *bread crumbs and Parmesan cheese, to taste*

DIRECTIONS

1. Place oven rack in bottom third of the oven and preheat to 400 degrees.

2. In each crust, layer:

    BOTTOM—Turkey Picadillo (fill crusts about ½ way to top)

    MIDDLE—Plantains in a single layer to cover picadillo completely

    TOP—Mashed potato to cover the plantains completely (the pie will not be flat—it looks almost like a big potato dome over the top of the pie)

3. Lightly sprinkle bread crumbs and Parmesan cheese on top.

4. Cover edges of pie crust with aluminum foil to prevent overbrowning. Remove foil approximately 15 minutes before end of cook time.

5. Bake in oven until bread crumbs and potatoes are golden brown (approximately 1 hour and 15 minutes).

GRACE PORTS
GLEN OAKS, QUEENS

{ *Chinese* }

Known as New York City's "secret village," Glen Oaks, Queens, sits quaintly right on the border of Queens and Long Island. Sitting on what used to be farmland, the 1.25-square-mile neighborhood is still home to a working farm and is also home to our guest Grace and about 15,000 other residents. For Grace, Glen Oaks is "near where I grew up in Queens, but my family was originally from Guangzhou, China."

Grace says that living in this small enclave of Queens doesn't mean there aren't food options galore. "Eastern Queens is about as residential as it gets before turning into Long Island. You'd think there wouldn't be a lot of food offerings, but we've actually got a decent selection. Closest to us, there's a thriving Indian community. The Queens County Farm Museum is just minutes away. There's a spattering of Chinese restaurants and supermarkets too. Just beyond that, there's a whole slew of Korean offerings, along with a recently opened Peruvian place. Halal carts, pizza places, delis, and a ton of other stuff—a lot of it within walking distance."

The large diversity of Queens is another asset that Grace loves about living in the borough. "Having lived here almost all my life, it feels as if Queens is a high-density international suburb with thousands of nooks and crannies serving authentic food from all over the world."

Living in a culturally diverse borough is also reflected in the variety of Cantonese recipes that Grace and her family have shared with us. "We made steamed fish, stir-fried greens, pan-fried chicken wings, squash soup, and clay pot rice. Both of my parents cooked, but my dad was the one who really loved it. He taught both me and my sister how to cook. Making dinner for the family was

one of our daily responsibilities. With the exception of the chicken wings (my father's own recipe), this meal is a typical Cantonese dinner for four. It's pretty much the kind of food we ate every day."

Since food was prominent in Grace's life on a daily basis, her memories of food as a child weren't so much a general feeling but more specific moments in time. "It's hard to pick just one. My mother used to make stir-fried crab for my birthday (instead of cake). I remember her trying to melt the wax on the bottom of the candle so it would stick to the crab's shell."

Grace's philosophies on food range from social interaction to something more spiritual. "I always think of eating as one of those necessary activities people can share. I have to do other things like sleep and use the bathroom, but sharing those activities doesn't sound quite so appealing to me. Not too long ago, I was struck with the realization that the Eucharist was food, and I couldn't get over it for weeks. Maybe food is something more than just physical nourishment or a vehicle for social interaction. My favorite forms of meal sharing are the ones that are highly communal. Hot pot, table grilling, shabu shabu, mookata, fondue. . . . The food is served in such a way that emphasizes cooperation and togetherness. It's also nice to have your guests cooking the food for a change."

The great thing about Grace is how she takes these philosophies and, in turn, views food as art in a simplistic way. "There's a lot of creativity in the world. Museums house works of art. Dance and music are performed everywhere. I think it makes sense to pass down the memory of tastes, sounds, and textures in the form of recipes because they carry a valuable record of human experience that speak to us in a way that are distinct from other forms of expression." Amazing!

Fuzzy Squash Broth

"I typically default to half chicken and half pork bones, but you can use any ratio you want. You can even replace the fuzzy squash with two stalks of scallion for a basic stock that can be used as an ingredient for other Cantonese dishes (such as the Stir-Fried Choy Sum recipe). If you can't find fuzzy squash, you can use other ingredients such as green guava, wintermelon, or carrots and potatoes." — Grace

3 lbs. bones, chicken or pork

water

¼ inch ginger, minced

2 six-inch fuzzy squashes, peeled, cut into two-inch cross sections

Salt, to taste

DIRECTIONS

1. Fill an 8-quart pot with the raw bones and submerge in water.

2. Bring to a boil and remove from heat.

3. Rinse off each bone until the scum is washed off.

4. Clean out the pot and arrange the ginger, squash, and bones so that they fit compactly inside the pot.

5. Fill the pot with cold water to just barely cover the ingredients. Bring to a boil and immediately lower heat.

6. Add about half the amount of salt you think you'll want in the broth. This will give the salt plenty of time to season the ingredients.

7. Cover the pot and let simmer for 2 hours.

8. Skim off any excess fat and add salt to taste.

9. Ladle the broth into individual bowls for each person.

10. Gently place the squash in a larger bowl for the table. The bones can be discarded.

Steamed Striped Bass

1 whole striped bass, scaled, gutted, and trimmed

Salt, to taste

⅛ inch ginger, peeled and julienned

2 Tbsp. soy sauce

2 Tbsp. water

1 Tbsp. sugar

2 Tbsp. corn or canola oil

1 stalk scallion, trimmed and julienned

DIRECTIONS

1. Place fish on glass plate. Bring about 2 quarts of water to a boil and pour it onto the fish, scalding both sides and the cavity of the belly. This rinses off any scum and reduces fishiness.

2. Generously salt the fish and let sit for about 20 minutes.

3. Place a steam rack in a wok and fill with water to just below the top of the rack. This would be a steam rack that looks like a stand for a plate. If you don't have a wok, a wide shallow pan with a lid will do. Cover the wok and bring the water to a boil.

4. If the fish is particularly thick, use a knife to cut diagonal slashes into the thickest parts. If the fish is cold, use the defrost setting on the microwave to bring it to room temperature (without cooking it) right before steaming.

5. Use a paper towel to dab off any excess moisture. Sprinkle the ginger on top of and under the fish. Stuff a little bit of it into the belly. Uncover the wok and place the plate of fish onto the rack. Cover immediately and set a timer for 3 minutes.

6. In the meantime, combine soy sauce, water, and sugar, mixing until sugar is dissolved. Set this aside for later.

7. Uncover the wok and check the fish. It is done when the flesh just begins to separate from the spine easily.

8. Remove the plate from the steam rack immediately and pour off any excess moisture.

9. Sprinkle the scallions onto the fish. Heat the oil until it is rippling and you see the first wisp of smoke.

10. Drizzle this hot oil onto the fish to scald the scallions. Ideally, the scallions will lose their raw metallic flavor but still retain some crunch.

11. Heat the soy sauce mixture until it starts to simmer and pour it over the fish. Serve immediately.

Pan-Fried Chicken Wings

4 whole chicken wings, cut into 3 sections

Salt, to taste

corn or canola oil

2 Tbsp. White Horse whiskey

oyster sauce

DIRECTIONS

1. Salt the chicken wings and set aside for 20 minutes. The wings need to be room temperature right before they are cooked in the wok. You can use the defrost setting on a microwave to warm (but not cook) the chicken. Dry off any excess moisture with a paper towel.

2. Lightly coat a wok or a wide shallow pan with oil. The wok should be large enough to accommodate the wings in one layer. If not, split the wings into multiple batches. Set the wok over high heat until you see the first wisp of smoke.

3. Put the wings in the wok and stir to coat them lightly with the oil.

4. Turn the heat down to medium, and cover the wok. Wait a couple minutes and uncover the wok. When the wings turn golden brown on one side, flip them over and cover again.

5. Once the second side has browned, toss the wings, cover the wok, and continue cooking until the meat is done.

6. Turn up the heat to high, pour the whiskey onto the wings, and cover again until the alcohol has burned off.

7. Turn off the heat. Add enough oyster sauce for a thin coating and toss the wings. Serve immediately.

Stir-Fried Choy Sum

"This recipe works with any variety of choy sum and with a few other vegetables as well (broccoli, mustard greens, and so on)." — Grace

1 lb. choy sum (Chinese flowering cabbage)

5–6 quarts water

½ cup stock made from chicken and pork bones

1 Tbsp. cornstarch

2 Tbsp. corn or canola oil

2 garlic cloves, peeled and crushed

DIRECTIONS

1. Wash the choy sum, separating the stems from the leaves and cutting them into bite-sized pieces.

2. Bring about 6 quarts of water to a rolling boil and drop in the stem pieces. When they start to turn bright green, add the leaves and submerge them in the water.

3. When the leaves start to soften (which takes only a few seconds), pour the choy sum into a colander and salt to taste. Separate any leaves that have clumped together.

4. Bring the stock to room temperature and mix thoroughly with the cornstarch to create a slurry.

5. Add the oil to a wok or shallow pan, and place over high heat.

6. Check the choy sum one last time and pat it dry with a paper towel to remove any excess moisture.

7. Once the oil ripples and gives off its first wisp of smoke, add the garlic and let it blister (but not brown) in the wok. Add the choy sum and stir continuously until it is hot and evenly coated with oil.

8. Stir the slurry very thoroughly one last time and add it to the wok.

9. Toss the choy sum to coat and cook until the slurry turns into a glossy and translucent sauce.

10. Taste the sauce; it should feel smooth and velvety (not starchy) on your tongue. Plate immediately and serve.

Clay Pot Rice

2 cups uncooked jasmine rice

water

Salt to taste

corn or canola oil

DIRECTIONS

1. Add the rice to a 3-quart clay pot (or any heavy bottomed pot of similar size) and wash it in several changes of water.

2. When the water runs almost clear, pour out all the water and fill the pot with cold water until the water is exactly level with the top of the rice.

3. Now add 2 additional cups of cold water. If the rice has been recently harvested (the bag might say "new crop" on it), use a little less water.

4. Add a squirt of oil and a generous pinch of salt. Set it on the stove, covered, over high heat.

5. Once it comes to a rapid boil, uncover, stir, and quickly cover again.

6. When the water comes back to a rapid boil, turn the heat down to medium low. As the water is absorbed by the rice, the sound of boiling will subside.

7. Following a brief silence, you'll hear a gentle crackling or popping noise coming from inside the pot.

8. Turn off the heat without uncovering the pot. If you don't hear the crackling, waft to smell the steam escaping from the pot without uncovering it. If it starts to smell like toasted rice (not burnt rice), turn off the heat.

9. Rest for 20 minutes with the lid on. Fluff and serve.

TOP (l to r) Gloria Fraczak, Timothy Fraczak, Dan Ports, Hope Ports, Grace Ports

PAULINA COLON
MASPETH, QUEENS

{ Polish }

To some, Maspeth, Queens, is a neighborhood that's just a little too out of the way, cut off by creeks and expressways from its bordering neighborhoods. There's no subway lines that stop in Maspeth, and a large area is covered by cemeteries. Not too many people ever step foot in Maspeth, let alone remember it's even there. Except, of course, its residents, who love the small-town feel the neighborhood retains even though it's just five miles from midtown Manhattan.

With a rich cultural history, Maspeth has long been home to immigrants from Poland, Lithuania, and other Eastern European countries, which is where Paulina steps in: "My husband and I live in Maspeth, but my family is from Poland."

Paulina loves living in this community. "Maspeth is a very residential and quiet neighborhood. It is mostly occupied by families and retired citizens. The main streets (such as Grand Avenue) truly represent the diversity of the town. You can find Polish stores, Irish pubs, Italian meat markets, Chinese seafood shops, American diners, and Spanish restaurants and bodegas—all within two blocks of each other. You know that summer is approaching once you begin to smell barbecue on every corner. This is a very close-knit neighborhood—definitely perfect for growing families."

It's no surprise that Paulina has a great collection of Polish recipes from her family that she was ready to share with us. She chose to start with a simple Polish staple that everyone can enjoy. "I made 'sałatka jarzynowa' or 'vegetable salad.' My parents taught me how to make it; however, this version of the recipe comes down to us from my grandfather. He substituted celery root for potatoes, making it a lot heartier." A traditional sałatka jarzynowa would consist of cooked vegetables—

Francisco and Paulina Colon

tomatoes, carrots, parsley root, and celery root—combined with pickles and hard-boiled eggs. All is mixed in mayonnaise and mustard along with many other optional ingredients, as you will see below. They key to the dish is that all of the vegetables are finely chopped.

While sałatka jarzynowa is a delicious but simple traditional Polish dish, Paulina remembers food being the centerpiece and entire focus of the holidays. She recalls, "My fondest food-related memories all involve holidays, especially Christmas Eve. In Poland, the Christmas Eve tradition requires families to make a number of customary dishes for supper, emphasizing this family meal over gift giving (although gifts are also part of the tradition). Christmas Eve is a fast day, which means that no meat products can be consumed, and only one full meal is allowed, so you can only imagine how exciting it is to finally be able to sit down at the table for the main meal of the day. While adults prepare the dishes, children are on the lookout for the first star (in remembrance of the Star in Bethlehem), which is an indicator that the meal can begin. Christmas Eve in my family was a very intimate day. It was never rushed, and we all got to participate in the meal making while listening to Christmas carols in the background. There was always a sense of peace and contentment (alongside burning hunger!) that surrounded the events of the day."

Even today, certain smells or tastes bring back and continue to create fond family memories for Paulina. "To me, food is the best memory-maker. There are moments when my mind is instantly transported to another time in my life with the simple smell of a dish, a spice, or a vegetable. Food creates conversation, relationships, and even traditions. It brings comfort and richness to my life, which is often stifled by routine. There is nothing like a satisfying meal at the end of a long day." A heartfelt explanation of the true meaning of food for us all.

Polish Vegetable Salad (Sałatka Jarzynowa)
Makes approximately 10–12 servings

The process of making the salad is quite time consuming. In order to speed it up, it is best to involve as many family members as you can, as long as they can be trusted with using a knife. In Poland this salad is always made around holidays. I cannot imagine Easter without it. Since it creates a great opportunity for family time, I recommend making the dish on a weekend or an evening when everyone can sit by the table and help dice the vegetables. My husband and I love this dish, not just because of its irresistible taste, but also because of all the fun we have while making it. The salad is usually served as a side dish to sandwiches, although it can easily be enjoyed by itself. More important, the proportions can be changed according to taste. My parents prefer the salad to be sour, so they add more pickles. My husband and I like the sweetness, so we add more carrots. Feel free to make it your own—there is no right or wrong in this recipe." — Paulina

NOTE: *"The following ingredients must be finely diced. That's the secret to this entire recipe."* — Paulina

1 small celery root (or a little more than half of a large one)

8 large carrots

1 large parsnip (or 2 small ones)

5 eggs

1 large onion

1 large apple, peeled (any sour kind is best)

1 jar of peeled, brine-cured pickles

2 cans of green peas, drained

2 Tbsp. of mayonnaise per serving

OPTIONAL INGREDIENTS

3 cooked potatoes, peeled and diced
NOTE: *They make the salad a little bit heavier so I personally never add them, although they are a standard ingredient in Poland.*

1 tsp. of mustard per serving

DIRECTIONS

1. Cut the celery root into smaller pieces. Peel carrots and parsnip (as well as potatoes, if you choose to add them). I usually cut them in half to minimize the cooking time.

2. Add celery, carrots, and parsnip (and the potatoes) to boiling water, and cook until they are soft but not mushy. Occasionally check each vegetable with a fork. I find that carrots cook faster, and I often remove them from water prior to removing the parsnip and celery root.

3. After removing all vegetables from boiling water, let them cool down.

4. In a separate pot, cover the eggs with water (about 1 inch above) and bring to a boil.

5. Turn off heat and keep the pan on the burner. Leave for 10–12 minutes.

6. Dump out the hot water, and then cover the eggs with cold water.

7. Let the eggs stand until you're ready to dice them.

8. Dice the onion and set aside, covered in a little bit of oil to help soften its texture.

9. Once the cooked vegetables can be safely handled, peel the celery root and begin dicing. Dice celery root, carrots, parsnip, apple, peeled pickles, and eggs, and place in a large bowl. If you choose to add potatoes, they need to be diced as well. The key to this salad is to chop everything very finely—not any bigger than the size of a green pea.

10. Drain and rinse the peas, and add them to the bowl. Add the onion and mix well.

11. Since this recipe makes enough for days of eating, I only add mayonnaise to the amount of salad we plan to eat at that moment. I separate about two serving spoons of salad per person for each meal. Place in a separate bowl and add about 2 or 3 tablespoons of mayonnaise. In Poland, it isn't uncommon to also add a little bit of mustard for those who enjoy some spiciness. Mix well and enjoy!

NEW
YORK

ETHEL
CORONA, QUEENS

{ *Guyanese* }

Ethel has an amazing story! She's so full of great stories about family, food, culture, and history that we want to hear it all in her own words. We want to live her experience through her memories and the pictures painted by the words on these pages and ultimately through the ingredients that complete the story in a warm, comforting bowl of Guyanese pepper pot. So instead of starting her story with her current life in Queens, we're going way back to the beginning.

"In precolonial times, the Amerindians in Guyana, still a major race there, created pepper pot with its main ingredient of cassareep for a number of reasons, but the most logical one is that they had no refrigeration. All of their dishes, meat-based especially, had to have a preservation method that also came from food or natural materials (smoking, preservative liquid, salting). This made securing food and cooking food both accessible and sustainable."

Thinking back to her upbringing in Georgetown, Guyana, Ethel remembers why she started cooking in the first place and why she chose to make a Guyanese pepper pot for this book. "I made Guyanese pepper pot. I say with reinforcement that it's a 'Guyanese pepper pot,' because there are a lot of Caribbean/West Indian, maybe even American Southern, versions. No one taught me how to cook this dish or any other dish. For me, cooking was a necessity, and that began at a very young age. There wasn't a real opportunity to sit back and reflect on my kitchen work and never the time to write a recipe down, so I have all of this stuff in my head—always at a ready in case someone needs to eat! Many of the dishes I can make Guyanese and otherwise. We didn't even eat as children, in my parents' religious observances, but, hey, you have to float with the crowd sometimes—so banned in my house was pork, but I can make a delicious garlic pork dish."

Jennifer M. Bernard, Ethel Bernard, Regina Bernard

It was at this young age that Ethel has one of her first memories making food for her family. "As a very young child, I made my first curry! I didn't yet know how to get chickens prepared for my father's favorite kind of curry, so I used potatoes he grew in his garden. I remember waiting for him atop our stairs and excitedly approaching him with my news. 'Daddy, Daddy! Guess what I made?' He smiled but seemed disappointed that it was potato. I was so very proud of myself that day. What a huge achievement. I was even more delighted when he and my older brothers ate it all. Maybe I was on to something then?" It's apparent today that Ethel was on to something—her amazing gift for creating amazing home-cooked meals, a professional in her own right.

Ethel reinforces her reasons for being such a great cook. "I always cook with love. Whether I have to, am rushed to, have all the time in the world to explore, am making small dishes, or elaborate and multiple meals, every single movement with my hands warms my heart. Everything is made from scratch and with love. My joy, however, comes when I see people bent over the dish I've made, and they pause to tell me how much they are enjoying it." The greatest compliment for any chef is the one he or she receives through mouthfuls of food.

Food is part of the fabric that makes up Ethel's life. It's become part of her living legacy, "Food means a lot to me. It's woven into my life from early childhood. Most people will remember their childhood full of play, frolicking outdoors perhaps, and other youthful activities. I remember cooking. I remember gardening in my father's garden, selling his greens to neighbors, cooking for my parents and all of my brothers before I was even an adolescent. I remember fishing, and back to cooking. After many years of all the meals I've prepared, I've developed a sense of happiness when I make a dish and can feed my immediate family or feed a stranger or entertain friends at my home with a feast all made by my hands."

Fast-forward to present day. Ethel is now living in Corona, Queens, but even her journey to New York City is filled with fragrant stories of family, food, culture, and a complete history of New York City. "[Our family] remixed in Hell's Kitchen, Manhattan, when we arrived to the States. Corona seems like a large place, but every corner is very similar to the other, and although I've lived here now seventeen years, I still have not been able to firmly claim it as my home. I guess because I spent so much of my arrival to the States in Hell's Kitchen—I still have strong ties to that place—my butcher is there, my dry cleaners for over twenty-five years is still there, where I buy my raisins for my black cake is still there. Corona is mostly Latino and Spanish-speaking, and I usually can't find my ingredients in my own neighborhood. There are an abundance of taco trucks, rotisserie chicken restaurants, fast food places, pizza, and other quick fixes. Just not my thing, I guess. I don't like someone else preparing my food in a rush—sometimes we venture out to neighboring communities like Jackson Heights or Flushing Queens and order out some Malaysian or Thai dishes, but that's as far as I'm willing to take my taste buds astray before I start needing to have my own food again. I can never get all my groceries in one place, so all the supermarkets that are around me now are just for small items (some milk, some tomato sauce, salt if we run out, and so on). Just as I did as a young woman when I arrived to New York, I venture out. I like to explore other places for ingredients, and new things to try. In Corona, you smell lots of fried food, and that's not a huge culinary tradition in Guyanese cooking, especially not in Indo-Guyanese homes. So I visit Chinatown in Manhattan that offers vegetables that are familiar and fish/seafood of all ranges, sizes, smells, colors, and textures. The smell of fish uncooked is sometimes too much for my grandson, but he likes to see them alive and swimming about on NOVA. I leave Chinatown, and when I lived in Manhattan, I would drive up to the Kips Bay/Little India neighborhood on the east side, and there I found curry powders, garam masalas, ground spices, and all the things that reminded me of my cooking time in Guyana. Now that I live in Queens, I go to Little Guyana in Richmond Hill (Queens), and purchase those kinds of Guyanese products there."

Queens does have a place in Ethel's culinary heart; her love comes in its "extremely diverse population of people and traditions—it's been noted as the most diverse borough in all of the five. You can find different versions of Chinese food (Szechuan is my favorite), Malaysian, Thai, Tibetan, Dominican, South Indian, Colombian, and Peruvian, and a whole host of other culinary traditions. You just have to explore. I guess other neighborhoods probably have varieties too, but Queens is the place you can actually find some level of authenticity in the kitchen and perhaps even ownership as well."

Ethel finishes her story with the reasons she's decided to take those recipes out of her mind, commit them to paper, and share them with her family, friends, and the world. "Without preserving this kind of tradition, especially in food—which produces so much history, culture, and dialogue—a part of who we are, who people are, and where they come from is lost, and if not preserved by every generation thereafter, it eventually becomes extinct. Migration has a way of forcing people to assimilate into newer culture, and it doesn't always become a positive transition. At least preserving traditional dishes within the family always gives everyone something to bind them together. At Christmas, no matter how busy my family is over the course of the year, we bond over the dishes I've made. My children, and even my grandchildren, my extended family by marriage (family who many aren't Guyanese), and friends, who are mostly not Guyanese either, all look forward to my dishes during special conditions. They help to reinforce how important my tradition is—so much so, that I can share it with them too. I also remind my adult children that they have to really know how to make something out of nothing—so all of these processes I've taught myself, and all of the preservation methods I picked up growing up in Guyana (salting, and so on) are priceless. Who can supermarket shop every day?"

Ethel's Guyanese Pepper Pot

"First of all, don't let the name of this dish deceive you. There is pepper in this pot, but it's not a spicy dish.

"This is a traditional Christmas morning dish. It's mostly eaten at this special time, but it's also a good dish to make when you have lots of people coming over. Whenever I host a small backyard summer party, this is the first dish to go, and no matter how much I make, there's usually not enough for everyone. Christmas morning is a great time to serve this too. It keeps with tradition and is enjoyed by many in such a special time like holiday spirits. I wouldn't recommend enjoying this dish alone—it's just not the same.

"The best way to bring out the flavor and tenderness is to engage in a slow-cooking process. [This dish is] very much a labor of love, and most people find it difficult to dedicate such time, so they use a pressure cooker to tenderize the meat. Perfectly fine!

"A note about meat: Really try to purchase meat for this and other Guyanese meat dishes at your local butcher or farmer. Stay away from supermarket meat if you can! Ultimately, grass-fed beef, and good-quality pork is best and keeps within the tradition of Guyanese cooking, absent of store-bought products.

"If you are able to withstand the aromatic smells wafting through your kitchen, then save your pepper pot for the next day! Let it marinate in its cooking liquid, and the cassareep will serve as the tender meat's preservation. Thanks to the Amerindians of Guyana, this dish never needs to be refrigerated either; simply leave on the stove and reheat when you're ready to serve." — Ethel

2 lbs. of oxtail

2 lbs. short (beef) ribs

1½ lbs. of beef (chuck is good)

2 lbs. of cow heel

1 lb. of best cut of pork (optional)

1 tsp. salt (table salt is fine)

½ lemon

1½ cups cassareep (Guyanese Cassareep from Pomeroon is the best quality)

½ cup brown sugar

2 Tbsp. dark soy sauce

3–4 sprigs of Guyanese thyme

4 sticks of cinnamon

4-inch long piece of orange rind

¼ tsp. freshly ground ginger

4 garlic cloves

3–4 dried cloves

1 onion, chopped

3 plump medium Wiri Wiri peppers

water

DIRECTIONS

1. Wash and dry all meat.

2. Place all your meats except for the pork in a large pot with water.

3. Add a pinch of salt and a slice of lemon, and boil for approximately 10 minutes to get the fat and raw odor off the meat.

4. Remove meats from pot and discard the boiled water.

MARINADE 1:

1. In a bowl, cover cow heel, short ribs, and oxtail with a generous coat of cassareep, brown sugar, soy sauce, salt, and 2 sprigs of thyme. Leave the marinated meat alone for 10–15 minutes so that the cassareep can seep through the meat.

   NOTE: *do not include the pork and chuck beef bits in this bowl of marinade. That will come later.*

2. Place the marinated cow heel, short ribs, and oxtail in a big pot and cover it with 5–6 cups of water (depending on the size of your pot) and let it cook for about one hour on medium heat.

MARINADE 2:

1. In the meantime, put together the beef (chuck bits), pork, the rest of the Guyanese thyme and enough cassareep to cover and coat the meat. Set this aside for a few minutes.

2. Return to your cow heel, short ribs, and oxtail being cooked and add cinnamon sticks, orange rind, ginger, garlic, cloves, onion, and Wiri Wiri pepper. Pop in your marinated beef and pork mixture.

3. Bring everything to a boil, and then turn heat down low. Slow cook until meat starts to separate from the bones. You can begin to bake bread to accompany this dish or cook a side dish, because this will take about 4 hours to cook. Don't abandon your handiwork. Keep checking for flavor and adjust as you prefer. If you're on the right track to pure delight, the cooking liquid should be dark and slightly syrupy when done.

4. While you wait, pour yourself one or two of XM rum and cokes, or XM rum and coconut waters, and tell "old time" stories with your company. Enjoy!

NEW YORK

AYA & REDD
ELMHURST, QUEENS

{ *Filipino* }

Aya first got a taste for food when she was young. She reminisces with a smile on her face about her childhood and the types of food she would enjoy with her family members. She grew up with many types of foods, thanks to an aunt of hers. She cherishes all those experiences. "My cousins and I would like to eat bananas with cheese for a snack or dessert. Also, my aunt operated a small canteen and we loved ordering snacks like burgers, tacos, spaghetti, chicken soup, fries, noodle dishes . . . that we never had to pay for."

Fast-forward to present day. Aya and her husband, Redd, both originally from Metro Manila, Philippines, now call Elmhurst, Queens, home. Aya started getting back to her Filipino roots through cooking and first learned a traditional Filipino dish called chicken adobo. "When I first moved here to the United States, I just experimented with the dish myself. Then when an aunt of mine visited from the Philippines in 2009, she taught me how to improve on my recipe." The end result is this simple yet flavorful version she has shared with us here.

Aya loves living in New York City. She especially loves her neighborhood in Queens. She loves the diversity in the people, the cultures, and the food. "We live in a quiet part of Elmhurst [Queens]. We just need to walk a little, cross Queens Boulevard, and we can find ourselves in the busy part of Elmhurst. I would say that people here at hardworking and quiet. The food is amazing. We have all kinds of Asian food, Latin American food, pizzerias, and Irish food as well! We also have a couple of good diners. I believe Queens has the most culturally diverse food compared to the other boroughs." That's something we also discovered while making this book.

For Aya, food takes her beyond just great flavors; it's also a spiritual experience for her: "Food is God's provision, a sign of God's love for all of us. Preparing food for my family is a way of saying I love them and I want them to be healthy. Preserving traditional family dishes is a way of keeping the 'Filipino' in my two girls who were born here in the USA." Preserving these traditions and cultural expressions through food is, after all, what *Real Food Real Kitchens* is all about, and Aya embodies that perfectly.

Chicken Adobo

"This is a very flexible dish, so you can really serve it for all occasions. In the Philippines, we would wrap the chicken adobo with some rice and tomatoes in banana leaves as individual meals. It's fun." — Aya

6 bone-in chicken thighs (you can choose whatever cut or parts you like)

⅔ cup water

⅔ cup white vinegar (better if Filipino brand, available in most Asian Supermarkets)

⅔ cup soy sauce (better if Filipino brand, available in most Asian Supermarkets)

3 garlic cloves, crushed

DIRECTIONS

1. Marinate raw chicken in equal parts of water, vinegar, and soy sauce plus garlic for about 30 minutes.

2. After 30 minutes, heat a medium frying pan on medium-high. Put in the chicken pieces. No need to put in any oil.

3. Pour in a little of the marinade, just enough to cover the surface of the pan and to prevent the chicken from burning. The natural oil from chicken will come out and serve as your oil. Just keep checking that the chicken is not burning. If needed, add some more marinade to the pan.

4. When the chicken is well cooked, add in the extra marinade, depending on how saucy you want your chicken adobo to be.

5. Bring to a boil, remove from heat, then serve.

Side Salad

NOTE: *this salad is made to taste.*

tomatoes

onions

cilantro

fish sauce (better if Filipino brand, available in most Asian Supermarkets)

DIRECTIONS

1. Dice tomatoes, onions, and cilantro. Mix together.

2. Add fish sauce to taste.

MANHATTAN | NEW YORK

Manhattan—it's the island everyone thinks about when they think of New York City. It's the cultural melting pot, the place that dreams are made of, like what Frank Sinatra sings of and so many people believe in: "If I can make it there, I'll make it anywhere." Home to thousands and thousands of restaurants and over 1.6 million people, Manhattan has hundred of food enclaves filled with culture and history throughout its approximate 33 square miles. With its population constantly in flux, Manhattan is, by nature, a global smorgasbord. Just exploring neighborhoods like the East and West Village, Harlem, Nolita, the Lower East Side, Chinatown, Little Italy, Spanish Harlem, Tribeca, and others, you're bound to find traditional cultural dishes that are as authentic as the people who brought their recipes with them to the city that never sleeps.

NEW YORK

NAKIA WILLIAMS & COREY RICHARDSON
HARLEM, MANHATTAN

{ *West Indian* }

Harlem is one of New York's most well-known neighborhoods. Every romantic image of New York City I have in my mind leads me to Harlem. The jazz, the poetry, the art . . . Langston Hughes, Duke Ellington, Billie Holiday, Zora Neale Hurston, Ella Fitzgerald . . . If I could go back in time and live another life, it would be during the Harlem Renaissance. I would slam poetry with Countee Cullen, start a zine with Richard Bruce Nugent, play the stage with James Baldwin, and write a masterpiece with Wallace Thurman, and then, of course, grab a late night bite of chicken and waffles at Wells Supper Club. Food and drink were always the centerpiece, the fuel to keep the vibrancy and innovation of Harlem pumping.

Today, Harlem is experiencing another renaissance, and again among the music and art, food is centric. A part of this new Harlem renaissance are newlyweds Nakia and Corey. Both work long days in the film and television industry, so when they have time to cook at home, traditional family dishes are key. "I made baked fish with butter and onions, and fungi. My grandmother from Tortola taught me how to make this. My family and I are from the West Indies. I am from St. Thomas specifically. My grandparents are from different places in the Caribbean: Tortola, Puerto Rico, St. Croix, and Jost Van Dyke."

Nakia loves the energy and vibe in Harlem. It's apparent when she vividly and describes what it's like to live in a neighborhood with such a rich history: "Living in Harlem is really amazing! It's filled with different cultures from all over the world. It has changed a lot over the years and has become a melting pot: West Indian, Afro French, Indian, Italian, Dominican, Puerto Rican, Mexican, and Soul Food can all be found in this neighborhood."

She continues with building excitement, "Living in Harlem makes me feel like I am walking in the footsteps of great and legendary people. I live six blocks from where writer Zora Neale Hurston lived. I live in the same neighborhood where Langston Hughes wrote his poems, where Moms Mabley performed, where jazz greats got their start. Harlem is an awesome place to be!"

With plenty of love and excitement for creating and sharing food in her new home in Harlem, Nakia also has plenty of cherished family food memories from her childhood. "I loved it when my father would break out the charcoal and makeshift grill made out of a tire rim and light it up outside. The smell of kerosene and coal would fill the house and ignite excitement in my brothers and me. We would instantly know that he would be making shellfish. . . . Once cooked, the succulent tender meat is so delicious. It's the type of thing that food dreams are made of. It was such a delicacy because of the lengthy preparation. My father would have to go to the island fish market, which was where the fishermen brought in their days catches. He would choose the fattest, meatiest fish and bring them home. The fish would need to be cleaned and seasoned and prepped for grilling. He would fill them with a salt, pepper, and garlic mixture, making sure to not oversalt them. He would then add a generous amount of thyme and onions. Then he would wrap each fish individually with foil. Now, they were ready for grilling!"

Food has affected Nakia on deeper levels in her life. It brought her and her husband, Corey, together. "My husband told me that he knew that I was the 'one' when I offered him a piece of chicken at a picnic. People show that they care about you through the preparation, sharing, and buying of food. Food is caring, food is shared memories, food is love. Food is not only something that nourishes, it's something that relationships are built on."

Those relationships that Nakia talks about are strong foundations in her life. They are the foundations that she built on to create who she is today. "The food I learned to cook as a child is part of my identity. Food connects me to who I am, where I'm from, and where I want to go. People should record their family dishes because it's a part of who you are. You immortalize your ancestors when you remember, cook, and document a family dish." All great things in life, be it music, art, poetry, or food deserve immortalization at the very least. Just ask the past, present, and future residents of the great neighborhood of Harlem.

Fish (with Butter and Onions) and Fungi

"This recipe is special to me because my grandmother would cook this for us as an after-school lunch. As a child, it wasn't always my favorite thing to eat, but as my palate matured, I came to really appreciate this dish. It can be prepared at any time really. It is a dish that will impress any dinner guest and will have their mouth watering for more. Here in Harlem, you can always find fresh fish at the local fish market." — Nakia

FISH

1 onion

2 garlic cloves

1 whole red snapper

2 Tbsp. sea salt and pepper or seasoned salt

5–7 Tbsp. butter

foil

DIRECTIONS

1. Preheat oven to 350 degrees.

2. Slice onion into rounds.

3. Mince cloves of garlic.

4. Season fish inside and out with salt and pepper.

5. Add garlic inside and on top of fish.

6. Place a sheet of foil in a baking dish.

7. Place your fish inside the dish on top of foil.

8. Add butter on top of fish. This will melt and coat the fish while baking.

9. Cover dish with foil.

10. Baking time will depend on the size of the fish. Here is an approximate time table:

    SMALL FISH: 30–45 minutes.

    MEDIUM FISH: 45–60 minutes.

    LARGE FISH: 60–75 minutes.

11. Fish will be flaky in texture when completely cooked.

FUNGI

1½ cups water

1 tsp. salt

2½ cups yellow cornmeal

2 Tbsp. butter

DIRECTIONS

1. Bring water to a boil.
2. Add salt to water.
3. Put yellow cornmeal into a bowl.
4. Add boiling water until it just covers cornmeal. You will have some water left in your pan.
5. Mix cornmeal and water together to eliminate lumps.
6. Add the cornmeal and water mixture back to pan, and bring to a boil again.
7. Reduce to medium heat and stir mixture.
8. Turn heat to low and continue to stir until it thickens.
9. Remove from heat and let stand. The fungi should fully thicken to a consistency like mashed potatoes or polenta.

RICHIE BIRKENHEAD

UPPER WEST SIDE, MANHATTAN

{ *Vegan / Pan-Asian* }

Since he was a child, Richie has had an eclectic taste in everything, especially food, and it shows in what he cooked up for us. "I made a vegan, Pan-Asian lunch consisting of pan-seared ginger scallion tofu, chana masala, Thai-style sautéed green beans, and steamed jasmine rice. I am self-taught. I've been fairly obsessed with cooking since early childhood and started cooking in earnest when I was in fifth grade."

Richie's culinary skills were influenced early on in life by both his mother's and father's sides of the family. Even though he has been vegan for the last twenty-five years, he has used those influences to create his own style of cooking, "I grew up experiencing two cultures simultaneously. My father is an English/Scottish WASP, so I grew up eating roast beef and Yorkshire pudding most Sundays, and I inherited his love of "colonial" cuisine like curry and dim sum. My mother is a Jew of Russian, Austrian, and French descent, and I have extremely fond memories of all the great European-influenced comfort foods from her side of the family. If I had to choose one fond memory [from childhood], it would be the first time I was taken to Chinatown for dim sum at Nom Wah Tea Parlor in the early '70s. My mind was blown by the vast variety of new flavors."

It's those flavors and influences that Richie incorporated in to the dishes he's sharing with us. "These are dishes I've cooked throughout the last quarter-century, and they've become family staples. Also, these dishes pay homage to my childhood. The chana masala is a nod to my father's deep love of Indian food, and the ginger scallion tofu encompasses many of the flavors every Chinese-food-obsessed New York Jew knows so very well."

Richie and his family are all native New Yorkers, born and raised, living on the Upper West Side of Manhattan. The Upper West Side has a creative vibe that Richie thrives off of. "My neighborhood is magical. I live on the Upper West Side, steps from Central Park, next door to the Dakota—one of the most storied and most beautiful buildings in the country. The Upper West Side has more soul than its across-the-park alter ego, the Upper East Side. While the Upper East boasts a high concentration of hedge fund managers, investment bankers, and CEOs, the Upper West has an inordinately high concentration of creative people. It is and has been home to John Lennon, Mick Jagger, Leonard Bernstein, Steven Spielberg, Joan Didion, Isaac Stern, Rudolf Nureyev, Paul Simon. . . . The list goes on and on. But, most importantly, the Upper West Side is home to a great many colorful, quirky, beautiful, and fascinating families. The residents of this neighborhood tend to be very warm, with a great collective sense of humor. Like most NYC neighborhoods, there are restaurants and shops featuring foods of every ethnicity and cuisine around the world. Perhaps the most iconic destination here is Zabar's. There is no other market like it. I went there recently and bought a jar of Frank Cooper's Vintage Oxford Marmalade, an assortment of fresh-baked bagels and bialys and an All-Clad saucier in one visit. Where else can I do that?" Upper West Side, here we come!

Richie has also been a singer and musician for a long time, which ultimately influenced his creativity in the kitchen as well. He's seen the food landscape change over time in a more positive way. "Being vegan and touring a great deal in the early '90s was challenging. The world was very different then. Basically, something as simple as soy milk was virtually nonexistent between the two coasts. I ended up devising creative ways to prepare vegan dishes and would cook for my band whenever the opportunity presented itself. It blows my mind that I can now walk into a supermarket in Kansas and find organic tofu, coconut milk yogurt, [and] all manner of vegan cold cuts."

For Richie, food and music go hand in hand, both creating a universal language among people. "Food is, absolutely, a universal language. The preparation of food is a loving, nurturing act. The sharing of a meal is a bonding, sensuous, intimate undertaking. It means nourishment of the body, mind, psyche, and soul. It means giving and receiving among loved ones."

As Richie finishes preparing his dishes for his family, he reflects on food and tradition and passing along this wealth to his children. "Tradition is of utmost importance. It is the life's blood of culture. You can't truly have one without the other. Tradition, along with creativity, makes us human."

(l to r) Richie Birkenhead, Jamie, Clive, Charlotte

Ginger Scallion Tofu

2–3 Tbsp. neutral oil (I use high-heat sunflower)

*1 lb. firm tofu, dried as much as possible
with cheesecloth or paper towels, then cut into
(approximately) 1" × 2" × ¼" strips*

*1–1½ cups chopped scallions (white parts cut small,
green parts longer)*

1 clove garlic, minced

1 tsp. minced ginger

A few drops toasted sesame oil

*2 cups any vegetables you want (goes great with
peas, snow peas, cubed zucchini, broccoli, corn,
and mushrooms) in any combination*

6 Tbsp. usukuchi or tamari

1–1½ Tbsp. mirin

1–1½ Tbsp. rice vinegar

DIRECTIONS

1. Heat oil in a large skillet or wok over a medium flame for about a minute. Tilt and turn pan to coat.

2. Cook strips of tofu until golden on both sides (be patient—it will take more time than you think, due to the high moisture content). Then remove them with tongs, set aside, and blot excess oil if you wish.

3. Add scallions to pan (add a bit more oil if necessary), and cook until almost starting to brown.

4. Add garlic and ginger, and cook for about 30 seconds, stirring and moving pan.

5. Add veggies and a few drops sesame oil, and stir-fry for a minute to combine.

6. Add usukuchi or tamari, mirin, and vinegar.

7. Add tofu, and fold together with everything to combine.

8. Add a bit of water, if necessary.

9. Cook, stirring gently, until veggies are just tender.

This dish goes really well with steamed jasmine rice and Sriracha sauce!

Curried Chickpeas (My version of Chole or Chana Masala)

3 Tbsp. vegetable oil

1–1½ tsp. cumin seed

1 large or 2 small or medium onions, chopped

2 chiles, seeded, stemmed, and chopped

2 tsp. grated fresh ginger

½ tsp. turmeric

1 tsp. ground coriander

1–1½ tsp. garam masala

½ cup chopped tomato

salt, to taste (I think I use about a teaspoon)

1 clove garlic, minced

5 or 6 cups chickpeas, cooked in a pressure cooker or a large pot (after soaking overnight) with a lot of water until very tender, OR 3 (15-oz.) cans, drained

1 cup water

DIRECTIONS

1. Heat oil in a large pot over medium heat.

2. Add cumin seed and pan-roast (don't burn it), stirring, for about a minute. You want to infuse the oil, so the fragrance should be very apparent before next step.

3. Add onions, chiles, and ginger, and cook for about 5 or 6 minutes, until onions are soft and almost starting to brown.

4. Add turmeric, coriander, and garam masala. Stir for only 15–30 seconds. Lower heat a bit if too hot (you don't want spices to burn).

5. Add tomatoes, salt, and garlic, and cook until tomatoes are soft, reduced, and almost starting to brown.

6. Add chickpeas and about a cup of water.

7. Stir everything together well.

8. Cook on low-medium heat, covered, for about 15 minutes.

9. Adjust salt to taste.

OPTIONAL: *garnish with a little chopped cilantro and lemon juice.*

Sautéed String Beans and Shallots in Vegan "Oyster" Sauce

3 Tbsp. peanut oil (or other oil if allergic)

¾ cup shallots, chopped

2 garlic cloves, sliced

1 lb. fresh string beans/green beans/haricot vert,
cleaned and trimmed

1 Tbsp. turbinado, or raw sugar

2 tsp. Wan Ja Shan organic shiitake sauce

1 tsp. Wan Ja Shan organic Worcestershire sauce

2 tsp. tamari

DIRECTIONS

1. In a wok or deep sauté pan, heat peanut oil on medium-high for about a minute.

2. Add shallots and garlic, and stir-fry until starting to brown.

3. Add the string beans, and stir-fry for several minutes, until they just start to soften.

4. Stir in the sugar, shiitake sauce, Worcestershire sauce, and tamari.

5. Stir-fry for several more minutes until string beans are tender but not too soft.

GAVIN VAN VLACK

EAST VILLAGE, MANHATTAN

{ Modern Mexican / Street-food }

Growing up on his own as a teenager in what was then known as Alphabet City, Gavin has pulled influences from his childhood to adulthood to create his current palate: a bit of the East Village back in the '70s–'80s mixed with his current careers as a musician and fitness coach, peppered with memories of his mother's cooking. "My mother was from Brooklyn, and her family came from Oaxaca, Mexico. I don't know much about my father except that he was Dutch, and his family hailed from Texas. I live in the 'East Village,' but as a kid the area was know as 'Alphabet City.' That was the section where the avenues changed from numbers to letters: Avenue A through Avenue D. I remember this old saying 'A, you're all right, B is bad , C you're crazy, and D, you're dead.' It has changed a lot since then."

Anyone who knows anything about New York City's East Village knows that it has a vibrant culinary history. It is known worldwide as the cultural capital of underground art, music, fashion, poetry, and more. Food has always been included in that icon of the East Village. Gavin recalls, "This neighborhood has changed and evolved/devolved over the years, but the culinary history is rich and varied. Back in the day, I feel it was much more colorful with Sixth Street between First and Second avenue being 'Curry Row/Little India,' and you would walk down that block just to breath in the air. There is still an awesome spice and sundries store there that I frequent for supplies. Life Cafe that used to be on the northeast corner of Tompkins Square Park (the musical *Rent* was based on characters from here) was an awesome spot to get a huge plate of rice and red/black beans for super cheap and was frequented by many of my friends in the squatting/homesteading community.

Two Boots Pizza that opened in the late '80s with their off-center concepts in pizza used to be banging and became somewhat of an empire with several citywide locations during the '90s, but it seems to have gone into decline. On Avenue C, there were two places in particular, Joselitos on C and Sixth and Casa A Dela on C and Fourth. Both had mind-blowing arroz con pollo with their own takes on spices and both at a great price point. Ironically, Joselitos closed that location and was replaced by a 'hipster' fried chicken spot. Don't get me wrong, they make good food, but it's at twice the price point with far less legitimacy."

Until he was thirteen, Gavin lived in the country. He recalls, "We were poor, so wild game was a regular thing, and we would broth down the bones. My mom was super creative about things, which she had to be with three kids on a tight wallet. I remember a neighbor of mine teaching my mom to cook muskrat, which I know sounds bizarre, but it was amazing. We're talking about a winter-bound rodent that lives off of dark, water-based greens. When it comes to pure 'source,' you really can't beat it. That and my mom could make awesome trout! She would pan roast it in the oven with whatever veggies were available and copious amounts of lemon pepper. This was usually spring/summer food, which sticks in my head as a great memory."

Today, Gavin's recipes draw on these memories as influence, but he also likens his culinary skills to many other aspects of his life. "My recipes are stolen from so many sources, and I also was born with a good sense of taste, so I kind of treat cooking like my music. I smell something and I start breaking down the components and algorithms of that taste because I like to think that taste, like music, is a frequency. They can be fun, laid back, seductive . . . so many different emotions. I have had some angry friggin' vindaloo!"

The recipes Gavin shared with us are important to him because "they both taught me to do more with less and make the best out of whatever cards you were dealt. Anyone who knows me knows that has been a constant theme in my life." This minimalist approach is apparent in these simplistic yet nutritional recipes. This is Gavin's modern approach to classic "carne asada":

"I am a huge fan of modified simplicity, so what I am making is my take on carne asada with kale and sweet potatoes. Again, this is a super simplistic concept, but the diamonds are in the details. Myself and the people I keep around me like to make food that doesn't just serve the simple senses but also fuels and heals, because in all honesty that is nourishment's primary function. The spices I tend to use are anti-inflammatories, thermogenic, and overall work as medicine. The primary purpose of food from being a 'survivalist' and competitive athlete is nourishment. Now, if you have the skills to make that nourishment really palatable, then it's a win-win situation. Also, food is great to commune around and is so much better when shared with people you love and those you hope to get to know. When you can gift someone with good nourishment and community, everyone wins. It's a lot like music." Good music, good food, good friends, and good conversation is what a great night in the East Village is all about.

CRAIG CHAPMAN

Sweet Potatoes, Kale, Guacamole, Steak

INGREDIENTS FOR ALL RECIPES

5 sweet potatoes

Coconut oil

olive oil

ground cinnamon

sea salt, grinder

1 large shallot

2 medium red onions

1 large bag of organic kale

ground powder turmeric

black pepper, grinder

8 whole avocados

8 large heads of garlic

¼ cup chopped, fresh cilantro

5 lbs. of grass fed skirt steak

butcher paper

cumin

smoked paprika

DIRECTIONS

SWEET POTATOES

1. Preheat oven for 10 minutes at 375 degrees. Cut sweet potatoes to preference. I prefer discs because they work well with the guacamole.

2. Rub each disc in coconut oil and place into baking pan. I prefer a pan as opposed to a sheet. Sprinkle semi-liberally with cinnamon and sea salt.

3. Bake for about 20 minutes until discs are crispy.

KALE

1. Preheat pan on medium heat with some olive oil to coat the pan.

2. Cut shallots and red onions into small pieces and put into oil.

3. Reduce heat to low and sauté for about 5 minutes.

4. Cut kale into manageable pieces but not too small; often you can buy it precut.

5. Put kale into pan. Season with turmeric, sea salt, and coarse black pepper.

6. Leave to sauté for 7–9 minutes. Do not overcook!

GUACAMOLE

1. Peel away skin and remove pits from the avocados.

2. Put 4 avocado pits to the side in case you need to store leftovers (although that seldom happens). Putting the pits in with the leftovers will prevent your guacamole from browning.

3. Peel and dice 1 whole medium red onion, and peel and dice 8 large cloves of garlic. Chop up about a ¼ cup fresh cilantro.

4. Smash the avocados into a paste, adding the onion, garlic, and cilantro. Do this in order for them to mix evenly.

5. Add salt and pepper to taste.

STEAK

1. Let skirt steak sit until room temperature.

2. Lay out skirt steak flat on butcher paper

3. Apply about 3 twists of pepper from grinder every 5 inches.

4. Apply salt the same way as the pepper.

5. Apply cumin, sprinkling approximately ½ teaspoon every 5 inches.

6. Apply smoked paprika the same way as the cumin.

7. Fold butcher paper over the meat and beat it with a metal or wooden mallet from end to end for 1 minute.

8. Heat coconut oil on low until it turns in to liquid form. Using a paper towel or cloth, sop, mop, and rub coconut oil into the meat from end to end.

9. Repeat steps on the other side of the meat.

10. Preheat an open grill for 5–7 minutes. Place the steak across the grill and let it sear for up to a minute before doing the same on the opposite side.

11. After searing, let the steak sit over the flame for 5–7 minutes on each side.

12. After pulling the steak from the grill, let it sit for 10 minutes.

13. Cut the steak across the grain to break the muscle fibers, and serve on a large service platter.

CRAIG CHAPMAN

THE BRONX | NEW YORK

Like most boroughs of New York City over the last century, the Bronx's once-quiet suburban streets have quickly given way to expanding urban development, luxury homes, and apartments, and an influx of urbanites looking for affordable housing. Probably most well known as "the birth place of hip-hop," and more recently Jennifer Lopez, the "boogie down" Bronx has also been marinating in food culture for decades. The Bronx's population is made up of a wide variety of immigrants who have brought a huge palate of flavors from around the globe. More than half of the approximate 1.34 million residents of the Bronx are Latino, and there are a growing number of Dominicans, Cubans, Jamaicans, Koreans, Vietnamese, Indians, Pakistanis, Greeks, and Russians. You name the type of food you want, and you got it in the Bronx: Puerto Rican, Vietnamese, Soul Food, Seafood on City Island, and more. Just take a long walk on Grand Concourse, and you will find it all!

TRAVIS WALLACE

MOSHOLU PARKWAY NORTH/NORWOOD, THE BRONX

{ *Southern* }

Travis was born and raised in the Bronx, a true New Yorker; however, he carries a little bit of southern soul in his heart and definitely in his taste buds, thanks to his grandfather. His grandfather moved from New Orleans to the Bronx in 1962, where he met and married Travis's grandmother. His grandparents then raised his mom on a whole lot of Southern food love, and she's since taught Travis how to use a little bit of that southern food charm as well. Thanks to his mother and the great dishes she has taught him, Travis continues the Southern food family legacy, a cuisine that can win over just about anyone. "Today, I made Cajun style shrimp scampi. My mother taught me how to make it a few years back during high school. My mom and I cooked together a lot when I lived at home. I moved out five months ago to try and be a big boy," Travis chuckles. "I find her teachings important to me, and they help me now when it comes to feeding myself and my roommates. My shrimp dishes are very popular among my friends, and I owe that to my mother. The thing about it is that she didn't force me to learn these dishes or anything like that. I picked up an interest by watching her and wanting to learn for myself. Do you have any idea how many dates I've successfully had thanks to her teachings? I thank her a lot!"

Travis calls the Mosholu Parkway North and Norwood neighborhood of the Bronx home. "My current neighborhood is very beautiful. I live right by two big open fields of grass, down the street from all types of food vendors and services ranging from diners and lounges to pizza and Chinese restaurants. It's a diverse community and very peaceful. Some delis have an amazing array of food that you can smell while passing by. This one deli in particular serves halal food, burgers, chicken

wings, and more. I went to go check out the lounge/bar in my neighborhood last week and ordered pan-seared salmon with scampi sauce. It was golden." It's always a great thing to have so many delicious food varieties right outside your door. Welcome to New York!

Travis is no stranger to the other boroughs of New York (except for Staten Island), but he has the most love for his borough, the Bronx. "I like to believe each borough has its own feel. Queens has the crazy road and street system that makes no sense to me still to this day. Brooklyn has been on the rise of expanding restaurants and bars that make the downtown area look like Manhattan 2.0. Manhattan just has so many options that the possibilities are endless. The thing about the Bronx is I don't always eat out in the Bronx because I mostly hang out in Manhattan and work there, but when I do eat in the Bronx, I have a few key spots that will always trump any other place. I think that's what stands out in the Bronx—that it might not look like there's much to offer, but there are these amazing hidden gems that make you want to always come back."

On a deeper level, this dish and the many others his mom has taught him hit him in the heart. "It helps you learn more about what made these dishes so special, and you can introduce friends or significant others to dishes they might have never tried before. It also opens the door for conversations regarding your family and cultural background. Most important, your favorite dish is more than likely to be a traditional family dish, so learning how to cook it is very beneficial. Food makes the soul happy. A happy soul is what I strive for." A beautiful goal indeed.

TOP (l to r) Travis Wallace, Christine Gonsalves

Cajun Shrimp Scampi

2 lbs. shrimp peeled and deveined

2 tsp. Adobo seasoning

1 Tbsp. Cajun powder

1 tsp. garlic powder

3 Tbsp. butter

1 Tbsp. oil

juice and zest of 1 lemon

2 Tbsp. chopped fresh parsley

salt and pepper, to taste

DIRECTIONS

1. In a bowl, toss shrimp with Adobo, Cajun powder, and garlic powder.

2. Melt the butter with the oil in medium-size saucepan over medium heat.

3. Add shrimp and cook for 3–4 minutes each side.

4. Turn off heat. Add in lemon juice, zest, and parsley.

5. Salt and pepper to taste.

Mashed Potatoes

1 lb. potatoes

6 Tbsp. butter

½ cup heavy whipping cream

2 tsp. garlic powder

salt and pepper, to taste

2 tsp. fresh chopped parsley

DIRECTIONS

1. Peel and cut potatoes into cubes. In a large pot, cover with cold water, and add salt to the water to taste.

2. Bring potatoes to a boil and cook until soft.

3. Drain well.

4. In small pot, melt butter and then gently add heavy cream and garlic powder.

5. Mash potatoes while warm in a large bowl, and slowly add in butter-cream mixture. Stir until smooth and creamy.

6. Add salt and pepper to taste.

7. Finally stir in fresh parsley.

GAELLE LOPEZ

PELHAM BAY PARK / MORRIS PARK, THE BRONX

{ *French* }

Pelham Bay Park and Morris Park are two bordering neighborhoods in the Bronx. They are known for quiet, safe neighborhoods to live in, meticulously taken care of homes and beautiful parks, and easy access to Manhattan. These neighborhoods are also a delicious cultural melting pot filled with food from Italy, Ireland, Greece, Germany, and many Latin countries.

Right in the midst of all this culinary diversity is Gaelle, a recent transplant to the Bronx from France, specifically living on the border of the Pelham Bay Park and Morris Park neighborhoods. For Gaelle, living in the Bronx is an exciting opportunity to take a culinary tour of the world and learn some new techniques to apply to her own cooking. "We are an international family. My husband José (called Jay) is American but from Puerto Rico, born in New York City. I'm from France. I arrived in New York City three years ago now like an au pair."

Gaelle continues giving a vivid description of her neighborhood, painting an almost magical picture: "My neighborhood, it's a very quiet one. You have small buildings, some houses. Two blocks away you have the Pelham Parkway, which can get you everywhere. You also have a bike trail; we love bike riding so it's just perfect. It's very green around us. I like it because even though you are in the city you don't feel like it. You can choose every kind of food you want—Italian, Chinese, Japanese, Mexican, frozen yogurt . . . it's a real melting pot."

Gaelle learned much of her cooking back home in France from her mother. She made a simple yet incredibly delicious traditional French family dish called "Carbonade Flamande," or beef and beer stew. "My mom taught me how to cook it. My mom (Nelly) and my grandmother (Arlette) taught

me to cook overall." Gaelle remembers, "Growing up in France I was lucky. My grandparents owned a big garden so all of our veggies and fruit came from it. Nearby, there were also mushrooms, hazelnuts, and walnuts too. You just had to go in the woods (during their season) to be able to find them. It was so amazing to smell the flavors, the real deal. I had my grandmother cooking a lot because for her (and me too), taking the time to cook for your family is another way to show them the love you have for them. I love to cook and share a meal with my family. It's just awesome."

These days Gaelle and her husband, Jay, cook for each other. She makes French dishes, and he makes Puerto Rican dishes, but they have also started a few new traditions of their own. "Jay and I don't really combine recipes. So far, we just give ideas to one another, like on the way to use spices (for instance, in France we don't use a lot of spices) and how to associate wine with a meal (to me there's nothing better than a red wine with cheese and bread or a dry white wine with fish or chicken, a sweet white wine with a chocolate dessert). We have some little traditions like cheese nights (we try different kinds of cheese with a fresh baguette and a red wine), or we have a crêpes party with friends (savory and sweet dough to eat with all kinds of fillings in the Brittany way)."

Gaelle and Jay enjoy trying to bring mealtime at home back in to their lives. Like many families, Sundays always seem to be the perfect time to spend shopping for ingredients, cooking, and spending time together in the kitchen. "I think a good time for people to create this dish is a Sunday family meal. Not for a celebration. It's a simple dish, a good one with a lot of flavors and tenderness . . . it's great to share with the ones you love."

For Gaelle, food is incredibly important. The memories of food she holds in her heart are what makes her passionate about food. "It's very important to preserve traditional family dishes because it's your family history; it's your legacy for you and your kids and your grandkids. I have so many memories associated with food and my family, like the traditional Christmas dinners with mushrooms I found in the woods with my dad, or my grandmother teaching me the way to make an apple pie when I was four with the apples from her garden apple tree. Did you ever walk down the street and think, 'Hmm, it smells like vanilla' and remember your grandmother, who was wearing vanilla perfume, or the vanilla cream inside of a strawberry cake?" It's these kinds of food memories that will last us all a lifetime. We can still smell Mom in the kitchen today.

Carbonnade Flamande (Beef and Beer Stew) *Serves 4*

"The secret of making a successful casserole lies in the choice of top quality ingredients. Prime beef suitable for long, slow cooking is obviously the essential ingredient, neither too fat and sinewy, nor too lean (chuck steak is the best cut to buy outside France). Use fresh vegetables and freshly picked herbs when available." — Gaelle

1 Tbsp. drippings or butter

2 lbs. chuck steak, cut into chunks

1 lb. onions, peeled and chopped

1 Tbsp. brown sugar

2 Tbsp. wine vinegar

salt and freshly ground black pepper, to taste

1 bouquet garni (a bundle of herbs tied together with a string: green part of a leek, thyme, and bay leaves used to prepare soups and stews. It is cooked with the other ingredients and removed prior to serving)

slices of gingerbread (bought or homemade)

hot dijon mustard

Belgian beer (dark)

chopped fresh parsley, for garnish

DIRECTIONS

1. Melt the drippings or butter in a large flameproof casserole dish. Add the beef, and fry over brisk heat until browned on all sides. Remove with a slotted spoon and set aside.

2. Add the onions to the casserole dish, and fry gently until soft and lightly colored. Stir in the sugar, and fry until the onions caramelize. Then stir in the vinegar, and scrape up all the sediment from the bottom of the casserole.

3. Return the beef to the casserole dish, and mix with the onions. Add salt and pepper to taste, and the bouquet garni.

4. Spread one side of the gingerbread with mustard, and then place on top of the beef and onions, mustard side down. Pour in enough beer to come just level with top of the bread.

5. Cover the casserole with a lid that seals tight.

6. Cook on a low-medium heat for 1½ to 2 hours.

7. Discard the bread and bouquet garni. Taste and adjust seasoning, and then transfer to a warmed deep serving dish and sprinkle with chopped parsley.

8. Serve hot with boiled potatoes or mashed potatoes or french fries (traditional way).

Gaelle and Jay Lopez

AVI WU

NORWOOD, THE BRONX

{ *Vietnamese / Japanese* }

Like many New Yorkers, Avi splits her time. She lives part time in the Bronx, goes to college in West Virginia, and visits her hometown of Ho Chi Minh City, Vietnam, often. "I'm a mixed girl with three different backgrounds: Taiwanese, Japanese, and Chinese, but I was born in Vietnam."

In the past several years, the Bronx has seen an influx of Vietnamese residents. There have been noodle shops opening up and down Jerome Avenue. That's a good thing for noodle fans like Avi. "My favorite as a child was noodles all the way!" Avi loves every aspect of the Bronx, especially all of the food options available. "It's an exciting city! Busy and busy. I like it—it's nice, and you can tell you're in the Bronx right away. Foodwise, I love everything, although I haven't gotten a chance to try Halal food here yet. I like sushi! Japanese food 24-7"

Avi's likes to experiment on her own, but she has staple dishes like the one she made for us. "Today I made a shrimp stir fry for dinner. My mom is the one who taught me how to cook. But sometimes I just like to go with my guts and just cook."

It was Avi's father's side of the family that first got her really into the world of food. "I got the passion for eating Japanese food from my dad's side. His mom (my grandma) is Japanese, and she made so many Japanese dishes. Since I was so young, I can't remember how she made it, but all I know [is that] it was delicious and amazing. She passed away when I was five. My family and I cook together sometimes still. It's fun and really good bonding together time."

While she works her way through college and finds herself far away from home, Avi related that the dish shared with us is one that always bring her back home. "This is my favorite and quick stir-fried dish when you're hungry and in a hurry. This dish will save you time and cure your hunger! It's also healthy for you, simple, and easy. It always reminds me of my mom when I cook it, and it brings out a lot of good memories."

Shrimp Stir-Fry

3 Tbsp. vegetable oil, divided

1 large onion, medium diced

1 large green pepper, julienne

Shredded carrots, to taste

¼ lb. fresh green beans, cleaned and cut in half

1 lb. shrimp, peeled and deveined

1 tsp. garlic powder

2 tsp. minced garlic

3 Tbsp. soy sauce

1 fried egg, diced up

salt and pepper, to taste

DIRECTIONS

1. In large skillet over high heat, add two tablespoons vegetable oil. Throw in onions, peppers, carrots, and green beans. Cook until tender.

2. Remove from pan. Bring pan back to high heat and add one tablespoon more oil.

3. Add shrimp, garlic powder, and minced garlic, and cook for 2–3 minutes.

4. Add soy sauce, veggies, and fried egg, and cook until all ingredients are hot.

5. Salt and pepper to taste and enjoy!

STATEN ISLAND | NEW YORK

S taten Island, the least populated borough of New York City, was once considered to be an Italian food heaven. However, the last decade or more has seen an influx of Sri Lankans, Liberians, Russians, and others moving to the island, opening up the city's smallest borough to a whole new world of delicious food offerings. This modern-day culinary makeup on Staten Island is reflected in these pages and is also part of the reason the island has gained popularity among New Yorkers looking for a greener, less-crowded place to call home.

NEW YORK

ROSEANN TRINGALI
ROSSVILLE, STATEN ISLAND

{ *Italian / Sicilian* }

Staten Island has one of the largest Italian communities in New York City's five boroughs, somewhere around 35 percent. This is especially true in the South Shore area where our guest Roseann lives. Over 75 percent of South Shore residents have an Italian ancestry. All demographics and numbers aside, Roseann's Sicilian heritage is a big bonus in our eyes and stomachs because she has shared with us a tried-and-true traditional recipe for Sicilian rice balls, a family favorite. Roseann begins her story, "I live in the South Shore of Staten Island in an area called Rossville. My family is originally from Sicily. My mother was born in a town called Alcamo, and my father was born in Castellammare del Golfo. The South Shore of Staten Island is mainly Italian-American. You feel like you're in Italy or in a scene from *The Godfather*! There are lots of imported Italian products, great Italian restaurants, and good people. There is no shortage of good Italian restaurants!"

Roseann's mother was a huge influence on her cooking. "Growing up I learned [how to make rice balls] from watching my mother make them. My mom always made us rice balls for our birthdays. It's a great meal for family gatherings or any type of celebration." Food revolving around holidays and family celebrations are always the most memorable, not only memorable because of the food but also because of the meaning and memories attached to that food: the smell, the taste, and, most important, the craft in making those dishes and the time spent together in the kitchen.

While rice balls are one of Roseann's favorites, they aren't her only memories of food from childhood. "My fondest memory growing up as a child is sitting next to my father and him feeding

me snails that my grandfather would mail to us in a shoebox from Sicily. My father would prepare them in tomato, garlic, and olive oil. They were delicious."

Passing on her Sicilian heritage to her children through food is incredibly important to Roseann, but so is exposing them to new cultures and flavors of the world. "To me, food is everything. Growing up in a Sicilian family strongly attached to tradition, food, and eating, it's all about passing on traditions. Also, my husband and I love to cook and introduce new cultures to our children. This is very important to us. It is a goal of mine to keep my Sicilian roots alive." Roseann has done an incredible job so far by preserving this traditional Sicilian rice ball recipe and sharing it with us. Enjoy! We did.

Sicilian Rice Balls (Arancini Siciliani)

RICE BALLS

5 cups rice (uncooked)

2 cubes chicken bouillon

3 Tbsp. butter

5 beaten egg yolks

1 cup grated Pecorino Romano cheese

MEAT FILLING

4 Tbsp. oil

1 small onion, diced

2 garlic cloves

2 lbs. chopped sirloin beef

1 (14.4-oz.) bag frozen peas

1 (29-oz.) can tomato puree

2 (12-oz.) cans tomato paste

2 tsp. salt, or more to your liking

2 tsp. sugar

1 tsp. pepper

1 package of fresh mozzarella (cut into small cubes)

vegetable oil, for frying

COATING

5 beaten egg whites

3 cups plain breadcrumbs

DIRECTIONS

1. Cook rice accordingly with chicken bouillon. After rice is cooked, add butter, and mix. Set aside and let cool completely.

2. In a large bowl, add egg yolks, grated cheese, and rice. Mix well. Refrigerate until chilled.

MEAT FILLING

1. In a large saucepan, add 4 tablespoon of oil, and cook onions and garlic until transparent.

2. Add beef, and cook until brown.

3. Add frozen peas, tomato puree, and tomato paste. Add salt, pepper, and sugar. Stir and cook on medium for about 30 minutes or until peas are completely cooked. Set a side and let cool 20 minutes.

ASSEMBLY

1. Place enough rice to cover the palm of your hand and make a hole in the center. Add one teaspoon of meat mixture in hole and one cube of mozzarella. Add one teaspoon of rice over meat filling, and form into a ball.

2. Roll in egg whites and then breadcrumbs.

3. Fill a medium saucepan halfway with vegetable oil and heat to 360 degrees. Add rice balls and fry until brown.

4. Serve with some extra meat sauce on the side.

photo by Rob Tringali

LESLIE ARRENDONDO

TOMPKINSVILLE / SILVER LAKE, STATEN ISLAND

{ *Latin Fusion* }

Leslie, a born-and-raised Brooklyn girl, currently lives in the borough of Staten Island. Often called "the forgotten borough," Staten Island should never be counted out as part of New York City's cultural past and present. Even though it's challenging to navigate (it's the only borough not connected to the New York City subway system), just taking the ferry to and from Manhattan is an experience in and of itself. It offers sweeping views of lower Manhattan, a close pass to the Statue of Liberty, views of the Brooklyn and Manhattan bridges and views of the almighty Verrazano-Narrows Bridge.

In Leslie's case, she lives in the thriving neighborhoods of Tompkinsville and Silver Lake, which are known for their amazing culinary scene. Leslie paints a picture of the community vibe in her neighborhood by saying, "It's probably one of the most diverse places on the island, and you can see it by just walking around. There are people from all walks of life, which is rare on the rest of the island. The people here are very family oriented. More people say 'hi' just walking along than in the other boroughs."

Leslie has a great love and appreciation for her own traditional family dishes. Her favorite to create are empanadas that include influences from both sides of her family. "My mom is from Mexico and my dad is Guatemalan of Italian descent. As a child, I remember smelling empanadas for every family party and running to grab one once they were done frying. This recipe reminds me of family and parties and just being happy."

For Leslie, empanadas are great to make for any occasion and can be filled with just about anything. They are quick and simple to make "for a party, gathering or even for a movie night, really for any occasion. I use leftover meats—just stuff them in empanada dough, bake or fry, and go."

Leslie carries a trait that many foodies have in common: the equal love of food, music, and culture. "I love music and food equally and it's reflective of my cultures, as a Latina, as a descendant of Italians, and as a native Brooklynite. I associate food with what I was going through in a certain part of my life, and those recipes have grown with me."

She continues this sentiment, "Your recipes carry stories of your loved ones and when you taste them, they are full of love, which is the best ingredient for any good meal. Food is culture, happiness, family, and festivity." We will be sure to share these delicious empanadas at our next get-together to carry on Leslie's tradition.

Empanadas

"The type of empanadas I make are rooted from the Argentinean version, but the seasoning I use for this version with meat is more Latin Caribbean. I really just fill them with anything I like, sometimes shrimp or chicken with chipotle seasoning, refried beans, vegetables, or breakfast versions with eggs, chorizo, poblano peppers, and cheese. I would describe them more as Latin Fusion." — Leslie

DOUGH

3 cups flour

6 oz. butter (unsalted and frozen)

4 Tbsp. water

2 Tbsp. vinegar

1 egg

½ tsp. salt

NOTE: *you will need an additional egg later in this recipe to brush on your empanadas before baking.*

DIRECTIONS

1. Pour flour into food processor and grate frozen butter into processor.

2. Begin blending, and then slowly incorporate water followed by vinegar.

3. Add egg followed by salt.

4. Once clumps start to form, turn off processor. Form dough into a ball, place in a bowl, cover with a damp kitchen towel, and put in refrigerator for at least one hour.

FILLING

½ red onion, chopped

½ red pepper

½ green pepper

2 Tbsp. olive oil

2 large garlic cloves

2 lbs. lean ground beef

Adobo seasoning, to taste

ground annatto seed, to taste

½ cup tomato sauce

Spanish olives (10–20, depending on how much you like olives)

1 tsp. capers

2 Tbsp. sofrito (optional)

DIRECTIONS

1. Heat a frying pan on medium-high heat.

2. Chop peppers and onions while frying pan is heating up.

3. Add the olive oil to the frying pan once it's hot.

4. Add peppers and onions to pan and let simmer.

5. Crush garlic and add them to pan.

OPTIONAL: You can add a good sofrito at this point if you have a recipe or can get your hands on a homemade one. Don't buy a store kind in the jar. It's not the same, and the peppers, onions and garlic give plenty of flavor.

6. Stir everything around until onions are soft and cooked.

7. Add ground beef to pan, and mix with peppers, onions, and garlic. Mix and break meat with a wooden spoon. Ground beef tends to clump, but for empanadas its best for it to be as fine as possible.

8. Once meat is mixed in, sprinkle Adobo and annatto evenly. Don't add too much Adobo because you don't want to overpower the other flavors and can always add more after it's cooked.

9. Add tomato sauce, blending into meat, and let meat simmer for about 10 minutes.

10. Chop the olives and capers, and then add them in.

11. Once the meat is cooked, turn off the flame, and let it sit till it cools.

12. Preheat your oven to 350 degrees.

13. Sprinkle counter with flour, and place your dough ball on it.

14. Pound it as flat as you can with your hands.

15. Add flour to a rolling pin, and roll it until it is thin and flat.

16. Cut out circles approximately 5 inches in diameter. You can use a large cookie cutter for this or any round object with edges.

17. Place the disks on the counter or a sheet of wax paper. If your counter isn't big enough, you can stack them with wax paper in between each one so they don't stick together.

18. Place about 2 tablespoons meat into the center of each disc.

19. Close the disc and seal the edges, and then crimp the edge with a fork.

20. Once you have completed building the empanadas, place on a baking tray that has been greased with butter. (You can use olive oil as well, but butter is the only one that truly won't stick.)

21. Brush the empanadas with an egg wash, and place in the oven for approximately 40 minutes until empanadas are golden brown.

22. Take them out and serve with your favorite salsa, guacamole, cheese, chimichurri, or any other fixing. Enjoy!

(l to r) Darien Cordero and Leslie Arredondo

ERITSA JONES
MARINER'S HARBOR, STATEN ISLAND

{ *American Fusion* }

Cooking has become a lifelong passion for Eritsa "Ritsi" Jones. Her passion for the culinary arts began at an early age, watching the women in her life bring dishes alive in the kitchen. It was the most magical room in the house to her. "I don't know if any one person taught me how to cook I would have to say that the influences in cooking styles came from my grandmother, my mother, and a host of aunts, who were top cooks in their own right. Then there is my own creativity. I've always loved pushing the envelope of flavors and tastes. My fondest cooking memory is when I was eight or nine years old and I took it upon myself to make part of the Sunday meal for my grandmother. Every Sunday, we made rice and beans with coconut milk. One Sunday, my grandmother was ill and I wanted to help. I followed all the steps that I had seen my mother and grandmother do so many times before and it came out delicious except for one thing: I forgot the salt," Eritsa laughs. "I was so proud of myself [that] I think I got the cooking bug since."

While she has staple dishes she's perfected, Eritsa thrives off trying new things and discovering new flavors in the kitchen. Her neighborhood in Staten Island, New York, has everything she needs to cure her culinary curiosity and then some, "My neighborhood on Staten Island is amazing, I love it! It's an eclectic neighborhood with all kinds of people—people of all races and religions and all creeds. I live in a neighborhood where all the stores that I need to buy all my cooking ingredients and supplies are so centrally located. The stores are a five-minute drive or ten-minute walk. I can find all sorts of ethnic ingredients, some that I know of and some for me to discover. That's my favorite part, the discovery. The food in my neighborhood is awesome. We have Indian food, Spanish food, Italian food, Irish food, Mexican food, Colombian Food, [and] Caribbean food. We also have those

street carts with the halal chicken right at the corner of my street, and they have amazing chicken gyros. The tastes and flavors of my neighborhood are amazing on the occasions that I don't feel like cooking."

Eritsa calls the neighborhood of Mariners Harbor on Staten Island home, but she is originally from Panama City, Panama, a city with a mixture of metropolitan flare and Old-World charm and rainforests. You can see both Caribbean and South American influences in her cooking. This is where the "fusion" comes in to her food. "Today, I will be making dishes that I call Sexy Short Ribs, Ritsi's Garden Salad with my homemade salad dressing, and Butter Love Butternut Squash Soup."

Eritsa not only loves the access to good food on Staten Island, but the community as a whole appeals to her as well: "The people in my neighborhood are friendly and eager to help. I really saw that during Hurricane Sandy—everyone pulling together to help each other. Staten Island is quite unique for being one of the boroughs of New York City. When you drive around my neighborhood you feel like you are in New England or something, with all the beautiful foliage that you see it's spectacular. Staten Island is not connected to the other boroughs by subway system, but Staten Island does have its own railway system. We are accessible through ferry boat and through the Verrazano-Narrows Bridge. Staten Island is the best-kept secret."

Eritsa likens food to art and spirituality and using food as a tool for the soul. "[Food] is a tool to nourish and heal the body. Food to me is like a canvas on which I experiment with flavors and colors and scents and textures. The possibilities are endless. I am a 'Culinary Artisan.' Food brings me joy, not in eating it, but in the preparation of a dish, or in selecting the ingredients for the meal I'm preparing. I use it to touch peoples hearts and souls. It's an icebreaker, it's a heart opener. After eating my food, people's hearts open up like the river." Eritsa smiles with certainty. "Food to me is the ultimate tool to bring joy to every person that eats whatever I've prepared for them from the heart. What I look for is the certain roll in their eyes that lets me know that they love my food.

"What I would like people to know about me is that no matter how much back pain I'm in once I don my chef coat and apron, it's like I don't feel any pain. All I see is the creation that I'm about to do. I love cooking so much that when I see that stove, I tune out everything else and just start cooking."

The final test for Eritsa's cooking came from her children, Natasha and Dereck. She passed their test with flying colors. "I have great kids. They never gave me any trouble about eating certain things. Derek's favorite meal growing up was liver with onions. He said he loves the way I prepared liver with onions." That's proof enough that Eritsa's cooking is right on point.

photo by Jamal Rolland

(l to r) Gabby Pascual, Andrew Jones, Charles Bowie, Gisela Pasucal, Eritsa Jones

Butter Love Butternut Squash Soup

"The dishes that I'm creating today can be created any time of the year, but our family mainly cooks these dishes during the holidays or for festive occasions. These particular dishes mean a lot to my family because the holidays mean so much to them. It's the most special time for me because it's a time that no matter what is happening in life, the joy of family and food creates the memories, memories that have stayed with me since my childhood too." — Eritsa

2½ lbs. butternut squash, cut into 1-inch cubes

3½ cups heavy cream

2 cups vegetable broth

1 tsp. chopped fresh rosemary

Pinch of ground nutmeg

1 tsp. pink Himalayan sea salt or to taste

Black pepper, to taste

DIRECTIONS

1. In a large pot on medium-high heat, add butternut squash, heavy cream, and vegetable broth. Bring to a boil and then reduce heat to simmer.

2. Cook until squash is tender, about 15–20 minutes.

3. Remove squash pieces with a slotted spoon. Place in a blender or food processor and puree. Or place in a bowl, and use hand mixer to puree.

4. Return blended squash to pot and stir.

5. Add rosemary to pot and stir.

6. Add ground nutmeg to pot and stir.

7. Add salt and add black pepper to taste.

Sexy Short Ribs

3 lbs. short ribs, 1-inch cut flanken style (ask your butcher to cut this style)

Season with salt, black pepper, paprika, thyme,

onion powder, and garlic powder

BBQ sauce

DIRECTIONS

1. Lay ribs individually on small sheet pan.

2. Cook for 45 minutes at 350 degrees.

3. Remove ribs from oven and then brush on BBQ sauce (I use my own Ritsi-Drew Que 21).

4. Put back in over for 20 minutes.

5. Take out, turn on other side, and brush on more BBQ sauce.

6. Put back in oven for 20 minutes.

7. Remove from oven and serve.

Ritsi's Garden Salad

6 oz. organic spring mix

½ cup crumble Feta cheese

⅓ cup dried cranberries

½ bell pepper (yellow/orange), sliced

DIRECTIONS

1. Toss in a bowl to mix.

2. Add dressing (recipe below) and toss again.

DRESSING

½ cup olive oil

2 Tbsp. Bragg's liquid aminos

⅓ cup freshly squeezed orange juice

1 teaspoon finely chopped thyme

1 teaspoon finely chopped garlic

DIRECTIONS

1. Mix all ingredients thoroughly in a bowl or jar with lid.

*You can reach Eritsa Jones to learn more about her cooking at www.ritsidrewcaters.com.

RECIPE INDEX

SPECIAL THANKS:

Darius Bass
Tory Clark
Melanie Cohn
Julie Coulibaly
Joy Doumis
Jeremy Hammond
Marcus Hatten
Ian Hunter
Jennifer Macdavitt
Gilat Metzler
Kristine Vera

Bronx House
New Life Fellowship Church

real food real kitchens
NEW YORK
COOKBOOK

ABOUT THE AUTHOR

CRAIG CHAPMAN is an award-winning television and film executive producer and lifestyle magazine editor. Mr. Chapman has worked for the past twenty years in New York City for MTV, VH1, Nickelodeon, *Seventeen* magazine, *In Touch Weekly*, Hearst Custom Publishing, and more. He created OEG Media LLC in 2010 and *Real Food Real Kitchens* is his first television and digital series. *Real Food Real Kitchens* is also a quarterly magazine and a daily blog. *Real Food Real Kitchens: New York Cookbook* is his first cookbook. He regularly speaks at the Center for Magazine Innovation at the University of Mississippi and his alma mater the University of Central Florida.

CRAIG CHAPMAN

real food real kitchens
NEW YORK
COOKBOOK

ABOUT THE PHOTOGRAPHER

JAMMI YORK is a photographer born in Queens and lives in Brooklyn. York is best known for his black-and-white portraits, street photography, and documentation of the hard-core music scene. Self taught, he has photographed countless seminal figures of the punk community and the New York City nightlife.